Just Like Nature Does

"Finding Happiness Through Gratitude
Empathy and Mindfulness"

Nicoló Di Leo Lanza

ISBN: 978-1-952263-48-4

Dedication

I want to dedicate this book to all the people who, during my journey, have shared free energy; facilitating the manifestation of this book. I say thanks to you as an individual although part of a collective of energies that combined together can bring to the light over the darkness, knowledge over ignorance. Keep on planting good seeds in the soil and be grateful for their growth.

Acknowledgment

I would like to acknowledge all the people who supported me throughout this book and those who evaluated every aspect of it. Those who believed in me. It is because of their constant support and trust that I was able to breakthrough and achieve this milestone.

My heart truly belongs to you.

Thank you.

About the Author

Nicoló Di Leo Lanza is a 22-year-old aspiring writer. Originally from Milan, he is settled in Melbourne where he indulges in writing and experiencing in nature's pleasures. This is his first book where he talks about the simple yet most marvelous things of life.

Preface

All of us like to believe that we understand ourselves better, we assume we have control over our life. But in all reality, we are clueless creatures, just killing time on this planet. Is this our purpose? Is this what we were sent for in this world?

I don't think so. Your purpose in this life and in this world is far greater than yourself. You, of all people, were born to do something bigger and extraordinary. Then why let yourself succumb to the distractions of the world? Why give in to the worldly possessions that are only there to put you off the pavement.

This book will help you understand your purpose and push you to make a difference in your life and this world. It will encourage you to move on and inspire.

Contents

Dedication.. i
Acknowledgment ii
About the Author iii
Preface..iv

Chapter 1 – Education..1
Chapter 2 – Mindfulness...23
Chapter 3 – Meditation 43
Chapter 4 - Starve Your Ego and Feed Your Mind...........61
Chapter 5 - Perception - Present Moment......................76
Chapter 6 - Move! 94
Chapter 7 - Our Brain..114
Chapter 8 - Give without Expectations of Receiving 134
Chapter 9 – Nature..144
Chapter 10 - Telepathy..163
Chapter 11 - Step Out of Your Comfort Zone.................180
Chapter 12 – Energy 198
Chapter 13 – Distractions 215
Chapter 14 – Communication.......................................231
Chapter 15 - Living with Sense....................................257
Chapter 16 - Acceptance and Forgiveness....................274
Chapter 17 - What You Really Need 291
Chapter 18 - Grow Your Garden 307
Chapter 19 - Love Out Loud...327
Bibliography 344

Page Left Blank Intentionally

Chapter 1 – Education

"Education is what remains after one has forgotten what one has learned in school."

-Albert Einstein

I truly understood this once I started living in Melbourne, Australia, away from my loved ones. I was only 18 at the time, and my mind was pretty open to new ideas, even though I didn't really know that until it happened. It was after my relocation that made me realize how inaccurate my views about education, knowledge, and self-actually were. I had to migrate to Australia from Italy for the betterment of my future, as well as the lives of my family members.

This meant that I was alone in a foreign land with no friends and nobody I could spend time with. What was even worse was that I wasn't even well-versed with the language. I could barely connect English words together and my pronunciation was terrible. This further added to my grievances, as it meant I couldn't really communicate with anyone. Looking back, I feel this was a blessing in disguise as it forced me into doing something I hated - reading books.

When I started reading books, it opened new horizons for me. I suddenly understood that books too could spark curiosity in me. It was this time that I enjoyed reading books, when they pushed me towards curiosity and would push me into opening the same book in order to discover what happened next. Books became my friends. They helped change my thought process, showed me the reality of life, and taught me what living really was. It was these new friends that guided me into a path that was above the average living standard, got me into looking at things that gave benefits other than those fulfilling the flesh. It was the first time I enjoyed reading, and then I was underlining and making notes and not because a teacher forced me and that honestly changed my life.

After that, I started reading a book each week and then I invested my money to buy musical instruments, like a guitar, piano, saxophone, and the electric guitar. I could see my brain changing, and I could feel that it wanted to expand more and more. I deleted social media, and that was the breakthrough instead of looking at my phone. I was walking around with a notebook and writing my thoughts or drawing. I took inspiration from Leonardo da Vinci. Reading books and writing changed me as a person making me discover new things, having new brain patterns and got me back to the curiosity that as a kid school took away. Before this, I was living a life that was full of ego. My ideology had always been so immature, very superficial. It was like all others of my age. I was only concerned about my looks and outward objectification, but the books I read taught me a different lesson. I realized that books were the main way that I could improve myself, increase my knowledge, and hone my skills to meet the needs of self, as well as society.

In my collection, I had a book about Italian inventors throughout history. Simply to pass the time, I began reading it regularly. This book about Italian inventors motivated me to become like them. My foray into books led me to change my lifestyle and the way I viewed the world. It wasn't simply my habits that changed, my entire perspective on various things took a turn for the better.

I started thinking why was I in the educational sector in the first place? Was earning money the only reason we gained knowledge? Wasn't it meant to improve our personality and help us turn into someone better? It was only when this thought struck me that I realized that getting a degree was only for monetary advancement for me. Look at it this way, what is the first thing that comes to your mind when you think of education? Learning, information, and knowledge is power, right? Wrong! If you ask a student what education is for them, they will probably make a face and start giving a lecture on their field – about what education is in terms of mechanical engineering, human resources, or aeronautic sciences; for example. This clearly depicts how badly the system has failed. Education has only become a means of learning skills that allow us to earn money and attain materialistic gains in life. In truth, education is a Latin concept that comes from the word 'educare,' meaning to 'train or mold' and 'educere,' which means 'to lead out.'

Both these words combine to form the ideology behind the term *education*. If you do an in-depth analysis of these two Latin words, you will realize that the whole concept behind education emphasizes that there is something, a kind of wisdom or intuitive knowledge that is already present inside an individual and only needs to be recalled or brought forth. In other words, humans are a huge source of information who need to realize how capable they actually are. They know what true knowledge is; which is why they are constantly in search of something more to learn.

The sad part is that education has turned burdensome for those who want to gain it. It is not only turned complicated in its acquisition, but it is also made stressful. Be it kids or young adults, all seem to be trying to escape the confines of what is defined as education these days. This is the reason why true learning is never attained. So, what are the issues that dominate education in the world of today? Here is what you need to know and overcome to become educated in the truest sense.

Learning like a Child

If I share my experience with my education, I have to say that all my years in school were very dramatic because I wanted to play soccer all the time. My teacher said that I was hyperactive and had distractions disorder. Now, I wonder how could you ask a kid to sit in a classroom listening to someone they don't even know for 8 hours? We are human beings curious to learn; we should be given the opportunity to learn around nature, going around experimenting things, climbing trees and finding the answers ourselves for the things that really matter in life. I am not saying that all the things they teach us in school are irrelevant but most of them are, and also we pick up this thing subconsciously where we must compete against our own fellow student to have a mark on an examination of information that you will inevitably forget. The point is they should teach us how to use our sense and learn with that instead of asking us to learn by memorizing and regurgitating information. They should teach us how to use our energies. How to be in the flow zone. Have you ever observed how a child is curious to learn new things? They are neither afraid nor self-conscious about how little they know.

Their thirst for knowledge precedes everything else. For them, every experience in itself is a course on education. So what is the thing that they have in particular and that we seem to have lost over the years? Curiosity. When you spend some time with children, the very first thing you notice about them is that they are curious about the smallest and the most mundane things.

Nothing is minor and insignificant for them. This is perhaps the reason why they seem to have answers to everything that even adults do not have. Another interesting thing about how children perceive the world is that they are open to experience whatever comes their way. They do not just wonder about the things they see, but also the inner workings of those things. For example, if they see a kitten or a bunny for the first time, they become wild to touch it, pet it, pick it up, and play with it by running after it. They do not care whether or not the baby animal has friends, feels happy, likes them, or wants to spend time with them. What do they gain from this experience? The ability to learn much more than any adult does. They have such diverse styles of learning that they garner more information than us. What happens to this curiosity when we become adults? This curiosity is pushed out of our mind as we grow.

The education system does not allow us to explore the things on our own. A student, in most cases, is never encouraged to question. Instead, they are forced to agree with how things are and adapt to them accordingly. Hence, over time, the curiosity to know more, explore more, and discover more fades away, leaving behind nothing more than a black hole that is expected to be filled with human-made education.

Therefore, there is a real need to maintain our fascination with the world and everything in it, just like children. How can we maintain this curiosity? By learning from visionaries such as Leonardo da Vinci, Albert Einstein, and Nikola Tesla. They're the people who never stopped asking questions or exploring new things they came across. It was their ceaseless curiosity that they are still known for. This allowed them to produce exceptional outcomes that are marveled at to date. Had they conformed to the education system that prevails, they would never have been able to succeed in life as they did. So keep them in mind when thinking of role models.

MOME(A)NT

"It's being here now that's important. There's no past and there's no future. Time is a very misleading thing. All there is ever, is the now. We can gain experience from the past, but we can't relive it; and we can hope for the future, but we don't know if there is one."

-George Harrison

One of the main problems of the world today is the distractions on the plate all the time. People, whether knowingly or not, refuse to let their minds wander. This results in a lack of creativity. Since they spend no time without having something in front of their eyes, including a cell phone or tablet or music in their ears, they are not living in the moment anymore. No matter where we are, even if standing at a bus stop waiting for the bus to arrive, instead of trying to focus on what is happening around, we usually remain occupied with these kinds of distractions such as a cellphone or tablet. By this, we seem to have an escape from the moment. When we do not pay attention to the ordinary and simple things in life, it leads to wasted energy. Creativity is lost as the mind is diverted to doing the things that are otherwise wiring the brain for monotony. From using social media to wandering aimlessly through the internet, getting lost in mundane criticism of self to openly regretting or daydreaming about material possessions, people just do not allow the creativity and artistic thought to flourish.

Social media, by far, has the worst effect on our psyche. It reminds us of all the fallacies we make and all the things we do not have. In simple terms, it asserts the idea that what we have is not enough. The platforms like these continue to feed our minds with what is nonsensical and non-creative. Instead of thinking about our betterment, social media turns our focus away and does not allow us to think in the greater depths of what the universe has to offer. Instead of wasting time on these things, it is more beneficial to relax the mind and focus our thoughts. Open the inner eye and think of all the possibilities that lead to the enhancement of ourselves.

Connecting with self would let us realize what our inner passion and hidden abilities are. We would then be willing to work for a progressive state that lets us dwell on the positive. Instead of remaining in a state of competition, we would more likely pay attention to how improvement within self can be made. Next time, when you are waiting in line instead of using your phone just have a little notebook with you and start writing anything that comes to your mind or even write something you are grateful for...

Keep your eyes open

As a general rule of thumb, we avoid realizing reality. We rather avoid making eye contact than casting a smile at a stranger. This causes us to become unobservant and thus leads to a lack of inspiration and creativity. However, this is not the only thing we miss when we do not pay attention. It could also happen that the love of your life passes by you, but since you are too busy with your head immersed in your phone, you don't hear them walk by. Would you really want to lose your love? This is something we cannot even afford to imagine. So, what can we do to increase our focus and better our observation skills? Here are a few easy ways.

- **Take a Walk:** Studies have proven that those who walk regularly increase their observation skills in a short span of time. This is the reason you might have heard that most writers, poets, and artists loved to take long walks in the mornings and evenings. The research explains that when people walk, they are automatically drawn to what is happening around them and are forced to think about a variety of things. This increases their level of creativity and also improves their memory.

- **Field Notes:** This may sound rather strange at first, but the more you practice, the more benefits you will see from this exercise. All you need do is select a place, sit there with a pen/pencil and a notebook, and write or sketch (whatever you feel good at) everything about that site. This will help boost the observation skills of your brain.

When you let go of observation and let your mind get cluttered, it is an invitation to the death of creativity. You stop using your mental faculties to think of newer ideas and investing your time in things that help open up your mind allowing you to think outside the box. This is the reason why it seems that the general masses are not creating anything unique or different. Everyone seems to be following the same path.

Only a few people seem like they are satisfied with their lives. Is there any way to take some time out from your hectic schedule and keep your creativity not only functional but also progressive? Here are some ideas to help you along.

- **Disconnect to Connect:** One thing that simply kills the creative thoughts in your head is the constant screen time you give yourself. Use of too much screen is not only bad for kids, but also for adults. Make sure you are not on your phone all day long and incorporate the habit of reading as well as writing in your life. If only you write what happens to you throughout the day, you will eventually learn to express other thoughts and emotions as well.

- **Pick up a Constructive Hobby:** This is the one thing that involves your hands as well as your head. From gardening to sewing, knitting to watching birds, you can select whatever suits your taste. These, apparently arduous, tasks instill a sense of focus and learning into your mind. You never know what might strike you like passion and get you involved in your own venture.

- **Remain Patient and Consistent:** This is essential. No matter what you decide to do to improve your focus and creativity, make sure you do it consistently for a period of time. Only then will you be able to see positive results. A few days or even weeks will not bring a remarkable change, so continue and wait for the change you wish.

Granting Right Direction to Energies

Recently, I have observed a trend and you might have noticed it too that people are more inclined to be involved in other's life than their own. Why is that case? From what I have experienced and from what I have had friends tell me in such cases is that their own lives are either too messed up or they are not interesting enough. This, I believe, is where problems arise. People start losing focus on what is real and what is not.

They begin to fall in the trap of the mundane and pointless activities. Our own lives should be the prime focus of how we manage things and what is essential to us. But the focus becomes everything that is irrelevant. It is essential that the attention is directed to what is relevant and energies are directed to the right path. By getting lost in the lives of others, be the people who are close to us or those we see on screen or social media (celebrities), we lose our touch with reality. Our own lives get lost in the background and we lag behind our own progress and personal development. When we do not keep our attention focused on what matters to us, learning ceases to benefit us. Our minds are always cluttered with irrelevant information that dulls our senses and renders our creativity useless. We continue to take others' word for everything instead of discovering anything on our own and understanding the potential of self.

Einstein rightly said, "*The fairest thing we can experience is the mysterious. It is the fundamental emotion which stands at the cradle of true art and science. He who knows it not and can no longer wonder,*

JUST LIKE NATURE DOES

no longer feel amazement, is as good as dead, a snuffed-out candle."

Understand this clearly; you cannot begin to comprehend what is mysterious until and unless you find it in your own life and with your own efforts. What others tell you is mysterious and important to them, as it is about their own experiences. Only your experiences teach you the real truth, one that is lasting and accurate. The whole point I am trying to make is that you should not believe everything you read or hear from others. You have to conduct research on the information you receive and then pick out the truth from the lies.

Broaden your thoughts enough to allow the benefit of the doubt. Let yourself grow as a person and make sure your life is full of questions that you answer on various stages. Let your curiosity remain as it is and explore it to the fullest. Do not kill it with confusion and lackluster ideas. Rekindle it with research and information that is current and has backing references. When you are certain of the information at hand, allow yourself to form conclusions. This way, you will be left with real knowledge - one that aids in growth, development, and a positive attitude.

True Essence of Education

We have already talked about how education is not doing what it should do for us. It has been turned into something materialistic where the only thing students seem to care about is the money they will be able to make once they are done with it. What is even worse is that they do not internalize the concepts they are exposed to, rather rote learning becomes the objective. From educationists to parents, no one seems to be bothered by the fact that education is not about gaining knowledge or improving the self anymore.

When I had not thought about it and was part of the mob mentality, just the idea of reading books would send me into a fit of boredom. I hated books and the idea of learning because they were forced upon me and did not seem to help in any possible way. All I could do was bother myself with concepts such as knowledge and wisdom. Stagnancy had become my personality. The only reason they have been giving me to read books and to learn was so I could get a positive grade and pass my exam.

Then one day, I read about the life of Leonardo Da Vinci. He just became the role model for me. He was the one who broke the norms and tried to study things that were thought to be irrelevant. And where did that lead him to? The discoveries that people still marvel at. It allowed him to break barriers and come across ideas that expanded not only his personality but also the society at large.

He is the genius who gave us not only arts but science that is linked to that creativity. It was only his resilience that led him to become a legend that people want to be and follow. It was Leonardo da Vinci's escapades in life that granted me the courage to step out of my comfort zone. As I mentioned above that I was alone in Melbourne, but the need to become financially independent and send money home was so great that I had to search for a job immediately. On my first day in Melbourne I woke up at 5 o'clock in the morning and started handing my CV to restaurants present in the Italian suburb. I did find the job but this job meant I was required to talk to the client directly. Confusion, fear, and embarrassment at not being able to speak English hindered my way but the books gave me enough courage to venture out of my comfort zone and become someone who was confident. My entire existence since then was centered on earning money. I was working three jobs, along with my studies and by the time I got home, I would be so tired that there was nothing left for me to do but sleep.

Three months went by like this and then I decided to quit. I accepted the fact that money was not the most important thing in life. What was even more essential was personal growth. So I invested in a few good self-help books and started incorporating newer habits in my life. These new books taught me that the sole purpose of education was to gain knowledge that does not only help survive in a world that cannot do without money but also helps to open mind and enable us to achieve ultimate heights of humanity. I realized that only through curiosity and its accomplishment, would I be able to learn anything that was worth learning.

I understood that the point of education was not to get the highest marks in class or graduate with the highest merits. Instead, true knowledge would allow me to expand my mind and grow as a person. I did not only become a reader, but learning new things helped me to step out my comfort zone more frequently and so I start trying to face my insecurity and talking with strangers even if I was aware that my English was terrible.

Then I signed up for a music class and started learning to play instruments, and also learned to code side by side. The books taught me to focus on my strengths, so I tried to add as many changes to my life as possible. It was these things that helped in the growth of my personality. One day, I decided to hit the football court and join the guys playing there.

After an hour, a man came to me and told me that I would be a perfect fit in their club offering me a contract to play football, I couldn't believe how could I have been at the right time at the right place? If you venture on new things, the doors of opportunity open for you all around. All the angry thoughts and the immature ideologies left my head and I was able to perceive things as others do and understood that there was so much more to life than living in the hell I was trapped in. I stopped rote learning and started understanding the science behind what I was being taught in class. I developed in myself the curiosity of a child who wishes to explore and is willing to understand, not just view objects critically. I let the learning burn into me.

Education became a tool that helped me gather the information that opened my mind. This is what we need to do. We need to let creativity roll out from within ourselves achieving the true essence of education. My curiosity helped me tap into all the potential I had and actualize them for growth in all manners and walks of life.

Your Doodle Page

Education helps people in unique ways… express, in your words, how education helped you in figuring out the way of life:

Chapter 2 – Mindfulness

"Mindfulness is the aware, balanced acceptance of the present experience. It isn't more complicated than that. It is opening to or receiving the present moment, pleasant or unpleasant, just as it is, without either clinging to it or rejecting it."

-Sylvia Boorstein

The idea of mindfulness originates from the ability to be in the moment, to feel present in its fullest form and to accept reality as is; without meaning to change it in any possible way. It can also be defined as the ability to bring back wandering attention. If a person is unable to retain their attention, or bring it back to focus, then they simply cannot be masters of themselves.

In the words of psychologist William James,

*"The faculty of voluntarily bringing back a wandering attention over and over again, is the very root of judgment, character, and will. No one is **compos sui** (Master of himself) if he have it not. An education which should improve this faculty would be the education par excellence*

(quintessential). But it is easier to define this ideal than to give practical instructions for bringing it about."

This definition and the above quote explain the idea pretty well. You are only truly the master of yourself when you gain the ability to garner your attention to address what is needed in the given time. This can refer to pretty much anything, from your education to relationships, working schedule to friendships, professional associations to self-connection. If you are not able to remain in the present and utilize it fully, then you are neither doing justice to yourself, nor to others.

According to William James, a good education should be able to make you capable of achieving mindfulness. It should make you aware of the faculties of your own mind, what your strengths and weaknesses are, and how you can control them in a manner that facilitates you the most. If education is not making things better, than it is not beneficial for you.

The reason why William James pays such importance to mindfulness is that it allows for character development and personality building. If you are able to control your mind, it means that you can do anything and everything you want to. I learned from my experiences that when I started reading, it opened my mind. I became more focused on the necessity of learning, because the new concepts I gained from my books didn't just keep my curiosity alive, but propelled me towards self-improvement. I was always trying to incorporate habits that would train my mind, body, and soul into becoming the best version of myself. It erased misguided concepts of ego, and self-worth and replaced them with humility, self-love, and compassion. I was able to burst the bubble that surrounded me and live the life that should have been lived all along.

Still not clear on what mindfulness actually refers to? Another way of understanding mindfulness is that it is a practice or mental discipline that is directed at training or retaining attention when needed. The entire concept lies on the basis that you need to be able to control your thoughts, emotions, and ideas when there is a need for it. Do you now see where the problem lies? It took me a while to understand as well, so don't get confused. Let me explain.

Importance of Mindfulness

Think of this situation where you are at home, surrounded by your beloved family. Even though you had dreamed of this happening and were trying for the longest time to make it a reality, it is only now that you were able to have the complete family in the same place; having the time of their lives. But what do you do? You constantly check your phone so that you are aware of what is currently happening to your friends, colleagues, or even random strangers through social media. Isn't this something you should avoid? Shouldn't your attention be focused exclusively on the loved ones present in the same room as you? Wouldn't it be more of an accomplishment if you gave all your time and attention to the people at hand?

The problem with our current society at large is that we are never in the moment. We are always trying to escape. Instead of enjoying 'what is', we are lost in 'what could be'. It's not that you are not aware of the party going around you, but you are not completely immersed in it. You have to know what is happening outside of that party, and thus you are unable to achieve complete mindfulness.

The normality has completely shifted today. I don't know how we got to this point where no one is able to focus on one thing at the time anymore! Our brains are hijacked so that we are always doing multiple things at the same time, while not really focusing on one. We have been led to believe that 'this is how the world and life work' – they fraud us into believing that is how we should also lead our lives, so that we can multi-task and earn more money? It should really be that they teach us how to use our energies instead of focusing on how to make money. Once you learn how to use your energies and breathe and be mindful then for sure your efficiency will increase and everyone as collective will be on the same frequency and vibration allowing the greatest to happen.

This is the paradox of time! We are physically present in one situation, but our mind is constantly diverted, traveling from one subject to the other. It is essential to understand that constant diversion does not let us feel things to their fullest and since our mind is casting projections all the time, they distort our real-life experiences of the moment. In turn, we are not able to fully absorb the experiences that we are going through and end up missing out on some important details.

Had mindfulness been possible for you, there would be no missing out on things that matter. It is through mindfulness that you are able to truly savor the experience of the current situation. It also allows for an attitude of acceptance, as by living in the moment, you choose that moment over everything else; thereby intensifying the encounter. I admit that reading this for the first time, I too became rather confused. Why was it even mandatory to go through every experience like it was your last? Why such an eminent need for forceful absorption? The thing is, without attentiveness, you let go of the fine aspects of life. If you are not paying heed to what is going on around you, you will lose touch with reality.

According to science, when you are in the moment, in the state of mindfulness, you are more relaxed, more attentive, and more peaceful. Your body is calm with low levels of stressors affecting it. Everything, from your blood pressure to your heartbeat, is regular which means your body is at complete ease. The mind, body, and soul exude serenity that allows for a sense of happiness and contentment. If nothing else, mindfulness leads to peace.

Remember, mindfulness is an exercise, it is not something that you are born with. It can be cultivated and increased with practice which means that you have the choice of adopting it at any point in time, so long as you are willing. Yes, your mind is prone to wandering and will continue to go out of focus from time to time, but if you have the power of mindfulness, you will be able to call it back to attention consciously.

How Does Mindfulness Work

Let's take some more examples to fully understand the ideals of mindfulness. Is your attention dwindling away? As I've said before, mindfulness is all about living with awareness, it is about taking charge of your thoughts and redirecting them to the situation at hand. Consider this. There is a musician who needs to learn a certain piece of music.

What will she do? Focus only on the notes that she is unable to master. She will be mindful of how the organ/instrument is being played and what she can do to improve her practice. This means she is only experiencing what is relevant for her in that particular piece of music because there is an intention to learn.

If the musician was paying attention to people around her, staring off into the distance, or simply enjoying what she was listening to, then she would not truly be in the state of mindfulness and hence would not be getting the essence she needed from the music. Similarly, a student who is studying for exams, suddenly discovers that he is going through Instagram instead of the book chapter he should have been reading. Without realizing what happened, the student had wasted 20 minutes of his time on social media.

Since he was not practicing mindfulness, he didn't consciously pull his attention away from Instagram and therefore, lost precious time. This is what keeps happening, not just to students and musicians, but to all of us at different points in time. We are not consciously and actively paying attention to the moment. As a result, we lose track of what was happening and become distracted. This is the reason why we take so much time doing simple tasks, because our attention continues to slide out of control. What is worse though is that we don't even realize that our progress is slowing down due to constantly shifting attention span.

The importance of mindfulness simply cannot be denied. It allows for development and progress because the focus is on one task only. The more divided your attention is, the less likely it is for you to get any task/assignment completed and that too in its perfection. Since your mind is not in control of the situation and not centered on what you are doing in the 'now', the results of your efforts will go wasted. It is through mindfulness and meditation that you can regain command over your thoughts. Once your mind is in reign, progress becomes inevitable.

Prioritizing Attention

You have to prioritize what is important when. Mindfulness lets you have an insight into what matters and how you can go about making it your priority. What you need to keep in mind though, is that priority changes from situation to situation. On one occasion, you may need to change the focus of your attention from one thing to the other, depending on what lies in the priority list. Sounds incomprehensible? The thing is, you need mindfulness to fully understand what matters the most, and where the primary attention should be.

Think of it this way, if someone is talking to you, having a conversation, is your priority answering them quickly, getting lost in thought, or listening to what they are saying in the first place? Truth be told, the matter of most concern here is listening to what the person is saying to you. It means you should not get lost in your own thoughts, nor be only worried about them to finish what they say so that you can respond. If these are your reactions, then you are not truly fulfilling the requirements of a conversation. You are not allotting the person talking enough attention or respect to truly pay heed to what they have to say. Revert your attention and listen with care.

Is the person trying to convince you, persuade you, get your opinion, advising you or simply want you to listen with an open mind? Once you have attained complete mindfulness, not only will you be properly attentive towards the speaker, but will also be able to respond in a way that satisfies them. With this new-found concentration, you will not just hear what the person is saying, but also be able to observe their body language, expressions, and the tone behind their voice. The responses that come from you after making these observations will be genuine, compassionate, and helpful.

Likewise, the example can be applied to when you perform other actions like eating. If you are not mindful of what you put in your mouth, then you will never be truly able to savor the taste and texture of what you eat. You will be too busy using the phone, laptop, TV, talking to someone etc. and miss out on many essential details.

Of course, this does not mean that there will be times when you are unable to give this kind of attention to the person speaking to you. You may have something else that is more important in your mind, you could be feeling low/high, or simply may not be in the mood to hear out what the person wants to say. From time to time, these things are inevitable and you must not feel guilty for them. However, you must ensure that this does not become a habit and your actions are not harming anyone in any possible way, including yourself. Never forget, inattention comes at a cost. Yes it is true that there are too many internal and external factors vying for our attention, so much so that maintaining focus or attention becomes a task in itself. This is why you need to train your mind to deal with these distractors and obtain mindfulness.

The easiest way to go about this is by segregating the irrelevant and the priority matters. For example, if there is some noise distracting you during your conversation, ignore the sound completely. The more attention you pay to it, the more it will affect your attention. Same is the case with thoughts. If you try not to think about a certain thought, then there is no way you would be able to stop it from entering your mind.

What you need to do is acknowledge the thought and then keep it aside to ponder over later. This way, your brain will know that it is consciously pulled away from the distractors. The trick is to make sure that you put your priority or what you are more interested in first. Let the distractors take the background and not hinder your attention span.

Mindfulness Everyday

As I have already told you, I was able to achieve mindfulness with practice. And if I can do it, I assure you that so can you. All you need is continued effort. The first thing you must do is identify your distractors, the default mode that turns on when you are trying to pay attention to a certain task. This can be referred to as your worried inside voice, negative self-talk, daydreaming, or merely a hindrance in general. It is this mode that bans our mind from becoming creative and productive. Remind yourself again and again that all negative emotions like anxiety, anger, fear and worry are distractors for the mind. They chip away at the foundation of real thought, leaving behind only that which does not let you progress in life.

Mindfulness, to me, is everything. We often don't realize how distracted we are, and we let technology waste our energy. Being mindful is keeping my eyes open so that I could finally see so many opportunities that were always there, but I was too distracted to see. You could have the next best innovative idea if you just are mindful of seeing it. Opportunities are always there; we are just blinded by the screens so we can't see it. Mindfulness helped me focus and become efficient in what I was doing and also took all my stress away. I wish I knew about mindfulness when I was a kid because I realized how many times I was lost in future anxiety during school examination. Mindfulness should be taught to everyone so they can learn how to focus and find the flow zone. So end it, deliberately and very consciously. Shut this negative inner voice and allow positivity to flow. Of course, stopping the thought in its track or making an effort to do so will not result in further reinforcement of the idea. Therefore, learn to observe these thoughts.

Let them come to mind, have a look at them, and then allow your mind to move on without dwelling on them for too long. Don't judge, don't cower, and don't label these thoughts. Pass by them, and you will experience a sense of freedom. Let these thoughts and emotions drift away like the wind because paying attention to them would mean that you lose your grasp on positivity.

It is this awareness of mindfulness that lets us discover the horrendous effects of negative thought. Had you not known about it, you would never have been able to remove it from your mind. You would have continued to live the existence of a scatterbrained person, with no real direction or goal in life. I was the same, so I know. Good news is, you are now aware. Since you know that these distractors are hindering your path and making you less progressive by coming in the way of your happiness, you can now actively work to attain mindfulness. You now have the tools to trigger the active and conscious thought processes within the self that will enable the exploration of a life that is focused, under control, and also worthy. You have the choice to embrace the presence of mind and get rid of that default mode.

Remember, the choice is ultimately yours. No matter what I keep telling you, or how much I may simplify the methodologies for you. Until and unless you are ready to accept what it is that you are missing out on, things will not change. Your mindfulness will only come out when you feel that it lacks in your life and strive to bring it in.

You remember how I told you about getting into football even though I wasn't? Yet it turned out that I was good at it and this is what I mean about mindfulness. You start doing something and later realize that mindfulness is involved, albeit unconsciously. Yes I didn't know I would turn out to be good at soccer, but what I did know what that I would try my best and put everything in it in order to do the best that I possibly can. My decision to work hard and produce the best results was conscious, and this mindfulness resulted in me actually turning out to be a great football player. I feel this is something that everyone can do. They don't have to know or chose something that they excel at, rather they can become engaged in any activity putting up their hardest energies and the mind will ensure you come out at the top. You can get involved in a way that your mind and heart is fully immersed in the activity so much so that you do end up becoming excellent at the task, whether you were before or not. And there is no better way to be mindful because once you are engrossed in the activity you are a part of, you get in the flow of things and any fears of failure or incompetence leave the mind.

This enables more than anything the success of the task. There is one more thing that comes with this kind of mindfulness. You learn to accept and forgive. This is something that I learned while playing football. If you have ever been involved in any kind of sport, or watch it, you would know that there is always some kind of foul or distracting tactics involved, what others like to call dirty playing. This happens and is pretty much unavoidable. The first few times that I was hit by the opponent team's player,

I was filled with anger and resentment at their attitude.

They would not only kick, shove and push, they would also pass snide comments and bully me. This was their way of pulling me out of my concentration, distracting my game. They wanted to upset me to the point where I wouldn't be able to give my best to the game. It took some time to understand and accept, but my mindfulness about the game was such that I was able to let go of this attitude. I grew to learn that this was nothing personal and the only reason the opponents were doing this was because they wanted me to lose, not because they had any kind of personal grudge.

Once the acceptance of the matter was there, forgiveness became readier. Instead of wanting to hurt them back, I forgave them, ignored them, and paid attention to my game only. This improved my performance dramatically as I no longer resented their interference and was only mindful of what I was doing at the field. I ended up with more goals as they were reverting to dirty tactics, while I was only aware of the game.

This I think is doable for everyone so long as they are able to continue to remind themselves of what matters, not the distractions at hand. I agree, this kind of restraint comes with time, but practice and you will notice the difference yourself.

And what is the best way to practice mindfulness? What was the one thing that helped me beyond all others? Meditation. It is effective, simple, and to the point. With being mindful I was thinking maybe share my experience with soccer saying that mindful is any activity that require your full attention so I was mindful without not even knowing it because it was very natural for me and so could be for anybody else when they are fully immersed in some activity that they are so focused that they lose the perception of time and they tap into a flow state zone that allows them to be extraordinary.

The second thing about being mindful that helped me was the forgiveness and acceptance that comes with mindfulness. In my experience, playing soccer taught me a valuable lesson in forgiveness and acceptance. In any game, all the two teams want is to win, and sometimes they use foul means to achieve that goal. I was often kicked by the opponent, sometimes to hurt and throw me off my game. However, I didn't once kick them back because I used to think with mindfulness. I was able to accept the treatment and let it go, focusing more on playing and scoring goals as a result.

Is Meditation Really the Solution?

Did you know that science has proven that people who meditate are able to control their brains better then you meditate, the prefrontal cortex comes into action and stops any extra thoughts from crowding your mind? This means that any stimuli that are irrelevant will not grab your attention and you will be able to work with full concentration. This was something that was tried with people who participated in a study and meditated daily for eight weeks. Afterward, it was seen that their attention span and ability to focus had increased considerably. These people were able to control the part of the brain that focuses, better.

Meditation also allows you to regulate your thoughts and emotions; helping you focus better on things you want. For most people, being able to concentrate on the task at hand is crucial since they are required to get a lot of work done in a single day. If you are among these, and your job or educational requirement is such that you need to get many things done in a short span of time, then this ability to control your mind will benefit you excessively. Studies that have been conducted at Harvard Medical School have also proved that meditation helps increase concentration, allowing people to control those areas of the brain that increases focus. This would mean that it isn't only your work or academic life that improves dramatically. With mindfulness you will also be able to flourish your relationships, whether they are personal or professional in nature. Have doubts about this theory? I suggest you read on because the next chapter is all about meditation and will help you with proper mindfulness.

Your Doodle Page

Mindfulness helps you develop strong relationships. Express, in your words, how mindfulness has helped you in in life:

Chapter 3 – Meditation

"Transcendental meditation is an ancient mental technique that allows any human being to dive within, transcend and experience the source of everything. It's such a blessing for the human being because that eternal field is a field of unbounded intelligence, creativity, happiness, love, energy and peace."

-David Lynch

This, I believe, is the true purpose of meditation - getting to look inside oneself. It is something that is becoming extinct in our current society. People no more have time to connect with themselves because they are too busy focusing on what is happening outside, the life that is taking place around them, instead of what is happening within.

It is important to understand what is happening within, something which meditation helps with. Meditation helps with the reconnection. It helps you find out what is within, without the intrusion of the outside. Confused? So was I when I first got acquainted with the concept. It was with time that I understood the real meaning of meditation and the importance of its practice in daily life. The question is, what does meditation mean? It is basically an action that helps with directing attention and energy to what is necessary. In this case, the most essential of all tasks is getting to know oneself, what are our thoughts, feelings, needs, etc. Only when you know your own self, would you be able to lead a life that is content, happy, and fulfilled.

Still not sure where this is going? Think of it this way, how do you get to know a person? You take time to talk to them, communicate about yourself as well as ask them about who they are. So how long does it take? Say a year of communication is when you can really say that now I know who this person is, what they want in life, what their dreams are, and what makes them tick.

In simple words, communication and time are what allow you to form a bond with an individual. You have to give attention to gain the information you want. Wouldn't you say it's the same with self? When was the last time you sat down and paid attention to yourself? If you don't listen to what is going in your mind, you will never know who you are. If you don't dedicate your time to yourself, you will never truly know who you are in reality.

The problem is, people are simply too uncomfortable with the idea of spending even a little time with themselves or any quiet time at all. Just the thought of sitting down and relaxing with no other distraction sends them into anxiety mode. Whenever such a dead moment comes up, they automatically pick up their phone, turn on the TV, or start listening to some music. And what does this do? It snaps their attention away from what is more important - themselves.

Did you get what I mean? This is something that you need to stop today, right now. You have to allow yourself some time that you spend just with your own mind and heart. Do not distract yourself the instant you feel you have some spare time on your hands. Transform the dead moment into an opportunity where you learn about yourself, become aware of your own thoughts and feelings, and acknowledge their existence and significance.

Understand this, it is in these moments that creativity is at its highest, seeping through your mind into your whole being. It is when you are bored that you will get innovative ideas and unique perceptions about what can be done. If your mind is constantly dulled by screens, you will never be able to think of anything outside the box or creatively. You will always be focused on the mundane and repetitive. The only way to break from this cycle of soul-destroying humdrum is to look inside. After all, it is your mind that generates all thoughts, shouldn't it be the star of your attention from time to time? Doesn't it deserve more attention than you give it? Only when you learn to be comfortable while being alone with your thoughts, will you be able to conquer your world. Become a witness to your thoughts and stop trying to chase them away with distractions.

Do not fight them, let them sweep over you and find peace in what you discover. You will be surprised by all the awareness you reach when you are open to your own mind. If you can get to know your friends through communication, there is no reason why you can't get to know yourself through communion with your thoughts.

Meditation changed my life a lot... I was able to let go of my ego completely. The little voice in my head that told me that tells everyone they are better than other people and always right – the ego that destroys relationships and friendships. I didn't know about the little voice in my head, was silently directing my thoughts and actions towards a destructive path.

Meditation helped me in finding and feeling the connection with the earth the universe and the energy I was surrounded by. This wonderful practice let all my fake ego desire disappear. To give you an example, let me tell you something. Since I was living in Milan, the environment I was surrounded brainwashed us to desire expensive cars, fashion and materialistic things. Since I started meditation, my focus changed and shifted on how to help other people.

Meditation also increases your energy and focus. Simple as anything you practice, grow stronger so if you practice how to direct your energies then once you have to do it, it becomes easier for you to stay focused for longer and also helps you stay creative. I have seen a significant increase and improvement in the things that I was writing.

As a kid, I was brainwashed that money is the most important thing, with meditation, I realized that energy is actually the most valuable thing, and how do you get more energy? With practicing meditation. As simple as breathing is a wonderful act if performed regularly with mindfulness. I don't like when people put a label on the word 'meditation' - I would just call it breathing consciously, or directing your energy.

Meditation Is Communication

When I was first confronted with the idea of getting to know myself, I had no idea how to go about it. What was I supposed to do that would help me reconnect with myself? It was then that I read and heard about meditation as a form of reuniting mind, body, and soul. The whole idea lying behind meditation is that you allow the influx of thoughts to continue without any kind of barrier. This, of course, does not mean that you let all kinds of thoughts hinder your daily functioning but rather you let thoughts pass through while watching passively, not getting affected by their intensity.

What's more? This way, you don't get attached to any of the thoughts that are going through your mind. You don't label them and neither do you try to get involved in any kind of way. The only thing you do is check to see whether or not they are productive and might help with healing or bettering you. This helps with finding out who you really are and what it is that you want from life. Remind yourself again and again that a thought is nothing more than an unreal projection of your mind, an illusion of either the past, present, or future. It cannot hurt you or change you until you let it. These trains of different thoughts should come and go as they please.

It is only when you feel that this train would lead to the right station, should you be willing to climb onboard. Did you know that a human mind has the ability to process and decipher somewhere around 50,000 thoughts a day? Since most of these thoughts are mundane and useless, it is essential that you learn to sift the important ones from the not-so-important and hold onto them. It is only we who can turn the volume down and not let every thought change our life or have influence over our decisions. We need to be in control of what affects us and what leaves without leaving any mark. This is the exact thing that meditation allows you to have - a semblance of control.

So, what did I do to connect with myself? I started keeping a journal. There is nothing better than writing to be able to access your thoughts in their full and final version. You will also come across undiluted and unformed thoughts that can be developed into something concrete that helps with your progress in life. What I did was I would write as much or as little as I wanted at the end of each day. I would keep my diary beside me on the bedside table and this way I would never forget to make an entry, no matter how tired I would be. There was nothing specific that I wrote. The only thing my focus was on was to let the stream of thought flow.

Reading my own entries helped me come across a lot of conflicts that even I didn't consciously know I was going through. Trust me when I say, writing down your thoughts and feelings is the best form of release and internal cleansing. It worked wonders for me and still helps me every day. Of course, this is only one form of meditation that you can incorporate in your life. You can take up walking, swimming, yoga, or simply sitting on a park bench if those are the things that appeal to you.

Meditation as a Stress-Reliever

The chatter that continues to go through your head, the voice of negativity hammering inside, do you know what it is or where it came from? It is the effect of stress that we experience daily. Meditation helps with erasing this negative chatter and improving the quality of thoughts.

Like I said before, creativity is at its peak when your mind is hovering around without any purpose. But the insistent stress of the day overshadows this innovative thought process and you are constantly bludgeoned without gloomy thoughts. With meditation, your mind clears up and there is space for original and positive thoughts.

You must have heard the quote, *"My bed is a magical place where I suddenly remember everything I was supposed to do"* but are these things productive? Ideas that help you to calm down or feel peaceful? Of course not, because you are so much under the pressure of the daily grind that all your mind comes up with is stress inducing notions.

But this can be controlled and monitored through the aid of meditation. You can decide what it is that dominates your mind. Meditation, or as it is also called attention regulation in scientific terms, is the practice that helps you control your thoughts. Breathing techniques or even lying in positions that help relax mind and body alike can give you the power over what thought flits through. You simply need to figure out which kind of meditative exercise works best for you.

What I am trying to accentuate is the essentiality of meditation in daily life. Meditation does not mean that you have to be sitting attentively or engaged in some kind of difficult yoga positions, you can be lying and still meditating. You can be sitting on a floor cross-legged, in a car, walking on a street, or literally in your office, and you can still meditate. This is the beauty and simplicity of meditation. It can be performed anywhere, anytime. Meditation or attention regulation or brain training, whatever you prefer to call it, can be as simple as sitting quietly - back straight so that you allow the energy to flow smoothly through your body - and focusing on your breathing - it is important that you breathe with your diaphragm, so place a hand on your belly and feel the air coming in and out.

Here is something more that you have to internalize. Meditation is not simply meant to relax you for a moment or open your mind for the time being. It is not a ten-minute practice you perform every day, rather it is much more. Look at the bigger picture, it helps you understand life and its various perspectives as they are and as they can be. You are building a whole new mindset within those short 10 minutes, more if you want! I feel that 10 minutes a day are not enough, which is why you should be practicing meditation throughout the day in short bursts.

Why? Think of it this way. You have decided to get healthy and since everyone always keeps saying how important it is to start the day with something healthy, you consume two carrots at the beginning of the day. The rest of the day though you eat up as much junk as you possibly could. But hey, there is no weight loss. On the contrary, you seem to have gained additional pounds. Now why did this happen? This was because you can't eat healthy once and then become healthy by filling your body with trash. The same is the case with your mind and meditation. If you start with 10-minute exercise and forget about the whole thing for the rest of the day, chances of your life changing your mindfulness increasing are little to zero. You need to ensure that your mind is not lost in the past (rumination) or in the future (anxiety trying to prevent the present). For best results, you need to practice meditation daily, throughout the day.

Keep in mind that this needs to come naturally and should not be forced because then the entire point of reducing tension would fade and you will only create more stress for the mind. I have noticed that many people run away from meditation because they are so determined to practice it mindfully that it becomes a burden they have to stress about, adding to an already strained mind. What we do is end up practicing anxiety, not meditation.

You don't have to force it on yourself, you only need to incorporate it in such a way that it doesn't feel pressured. This is the reason why you need to be sure that meditation is always something that comes naturally and allows you to relax, not become more aggravated. Another important thing is the frequency of meditation. It is important that meditation is performed in short bursts throughout the day. This means that you start your day with some kind of meditation, depending on what you feel most comfortable with. It doesn't have to be too long, just 10-15 minutes will do. Start of the day and end of the day are two best times as they encourage the release of energy and conversion of all the negatives into positives.

What you have to stress is the regularity of the act. If you miss out days, then your therapy is not going to work well. So commit to the habit and try to practice it at the same time every day. Within a short period of time, it will become like breathing to you and you won't have to mindfully practice meditation.

Meditation Leads to Enhanced Focus

If there is one essential thing that we seem to be missing out on, it is the focus. People have become so tuned to multitasking that they do not pay all of their mind and attention to any one activity. This leads to nothing getting done well. Think of it this way, when you are driving to work, instead of using this time to introspect or notice the things outside, we immerse our brain in music or news. The idea, of course, is to escape any kind of thought process.

Hence, the reason why there seems to be a rise in road accidents. We just do not want to pay attention to what it is we are doing at the moment, in this case, driving. When I first read about meditation, I loved the fact that all I was asked to do was to breathe consciously. So what I ask here is not to breathe for survival but breathe to excel. I fell in love with meditation straight away because if you think about it, it is a paradox that they took our superpower away - our ability to find the tune with ourselves, meditation just allow you to find the right tune.

You know when you listen to the radio, and the sound is off, that's how we sound when we don't meditate. Mediation let allows your real self to come out and really for me it was a huge discovery. Thanks to meditation I discovered a lot of new things that I liked and also I shifted my perception when I changed my way of living.

Meditation allows you to feel the energy within and utilize it in the best possible manner. With consistent meditation practice, you will be able to see life as is and not how it was or how it could be. You begin to notice where your energies are being wasted, how mundane things are causing distractions, and where your true potential is getting lost.

Try something else. When you breathe today, notice what it feels like. Pay attention to the movement of your body, the effect of oxygen going in and carbon dioxide coming out. Close your eyes and open your ears. Listen and feel. Let the energy flow from your spine to the head and from there to every tip of your body.

Let me warn you, your mind will continuously pull at your body. It will try to distract you, filling you up with thoughts that are useless, or even if they are functional, not really needed in that moment. This is where control or focus comes in the picture. Can you truly master your mind by reverting it toward your breathing pattern? Or do you possess no such control? If you can't focus on something as simple as breathing, accept the fact that you are no longer in control of your mind.

This is something you should be worried about. Why have you lost control? How can you regain this focus? The answer is simple, through meditation. Meditation allows for the opening of the mind and letting go of everything that does not concern you. Now the question here is, how can you have control on your mind? What I did was start by identifying the problems that were bugging me. What are the first few things when you think of the words *stress*, *worry*, and *anxiety*? Make a list because these are the things dominating your mind, causing you to lose control. Once you have gotten attuned to these issues, you can work effectively letting them go one by one. Another thing that is going to help you out is by understanding the fact that your mind is just one aspect of you - a powerful one that allows you to think, make plans, and generally command life. It does not rule you, you rule it. The minute you feel this power shift, you will be able to have a semblance of clarity. Yes, you have never been taught how to use your mind to the best, but it is something that you can master with a little change of tactics.

So long as you are willing to learn, controlling your mind isn't impossible. You just have to let some new ways to overcome the old ones. Hear me loud and clear, technology is the number one reason why you are unable to focus and control your mind. Our brain is not meant to multitask all the time. It is meant to be pivoted on a single point before moving on to something else. Whenever you try to do more than one thing at a time, it results in your brain making rapid switches from one point to another. This leads to a diluted concentration and you end up performing anything badly.

Therefore, dedicate your mind to a single task, do it with full attention, and then watch it bloom and transform right before your eyes. Do not let any kind of distraction take your focus away. Yes, this will take some time to adjust, but you will master this art so long as you practice it every day with determination.

Scientific Study on Meditation

Science has proved time and again that concentration can be attained with meditation. But proper attention to exercise and practice is required to make meditation mindful and unconscious. According to a research that appears in Psychiatry Research: Neuroimaging, conducted by Massachusetts General Hospital, meditation changes the gray matter inside our brain.

It was performed on 16 participants whose magnetic resonance (MR) images were taken of the brain, two weeks before and after they took part in an eight-week Mindfulness-Based Stress Reduction (MBSR) program at the University of Massachusetts Center for Mindfulness. The participants attended weekly meetings of mindful meditation along with listening to audio recordings for guided meditation practice.

This meant that the group spent somewhere around 27 minutes every day doing mindful exercises. When they were given a questionnaire, their improvements were clearly evident. The MRIs showed an increase in gray matter density, which is responsible for learning memory, self-awareness, introspection, and compassion.

This further proves the point that with meditation, you are better in control of self, know what you want, and become more comfortable as well as peaceful with your share of life. Hence, the reason why meditation can literally change your life.

Your Doodle Page

Meditation comforts you and allows you to take control over yourself... list the ways in which meditation has improved your quality of life:

Chapter 4 - Starve Your Ego and Feed Your Mind

"The ego is only an illusion, but a very influential one. Letting the ego-illusion become your identity can prevent you from knowing your true self. Ego, the false idea of believing that you are what you have or what you do, is a backward way of assessing and living life."

-Wayne Dyer

Think how fortunate you are to be alive and to possess the potential to create the life you want to live. I feel that too. But at times, it feels impossible due to the overpowering stress and frustration that seem to take over our lives. Did you ever stop and ask, how can my life be so different at times and what can I do to tap into my full potential and experience the peace and calmness in my life?

Eventually, it comes down to whether you choose to live your life surrendering to the demands and delusions of your ego or make the mindful intention to align yourself with an infinite mind. Choosing to live according to the soul gives you an infinite amount of possibilities, peace, passion, and purpose that you deserve and that you've wanted for a long time. On the other hand, living unaware and giving in your ego result in anxiety, unnecessary resistance, stress, and many undesirable consequences that you never asked for. I believe, as a unique and amazing human being, you deserve much more than what your ego offers you. See, you have basically two options to choose from and I'm sure you want what the soul has in stock for you. For that, you must discover your inner self and decide between the two.

Mindful living gives you complete peace and infinite potential, while ego and self-centeredness surround you with stress and the mediocre life that you keep seeking to surpass. Anything that makes me stay in the flow zone so when I write, when I play football, when I sing or rap or having a meaningful conversation, and most importantly when I help people.

Feeding my soul with real action staying around nature and climbing trees writing poems is what real mindfulness and soulfulness are all about. To be honest, I don't think any of us desires to live according to our ego. I believe we get used to living this way throughout our lives and never really realize there are more effective solutions.

The phrase 'I am' sets you up for false identification and future situations of depression and anxiety. It is this type of false identification that has the ability to lock you in one role. It, therefore, limits the vision you have for yourself and, in return, prevents you from experiencing life. Depression is a consequence of having a false identity that does not fit you and is hard to let go of. This false identity is based on your ego.

The real problem occurs when the value of self is attached to the ego. For example, you lose a job that made you feel important. You fall into depression because your feelings of value and importance were attached to your job. This also happens a lot when people break up, lose their dream job, retire, or face a major change in life that is the main cause of their ego.

"Depression is a process of expanding consciousness through spiritual awareness and growth."

-Amarjit Singh

Imagine a baby crying because its teeth are growing through the gums. Once the teeth are grown, the baby feels stronger and can easily participate in life's experiences more enthusiastically by eating a wider range of foods. This is a part of growing up in life. However, relating to the thoughts that contribute to your ego prevents you from growing in life.

You see, how you picture yourself sets your path. You look in the mirror and perceive yourself in a specific way. Then, your actions fall in accordance with the idealistic picture of yourself that is created in your mind. This is the reason that the more limited idea you have of yourself, the less diverse your experiences in life will be. In my personal experience, I feel thankful to meditation that the voice that kept me away to find my real self, that distortion, that sound was all gone.

I used to dream and desire all the material things - the cars, the villa, and fame, having people recognize me and congratulate me. All thanks to meditation, my real self-embraced me, and now I dream about bringing this planet back to life, bringing people to their real tune. All I dream about now is how to help other people find their real self so that then they can help others as well. And we all can live in a collective of creative individuals that by leaving their ego apart can use their energy to collaborate together and make the most beautiful art scenery ever.

What Is Ego?

Ego is a small voice in the back of your head that is always trying to analyze or judge whatever is going in your life or around you. Every time you think about the past regretting your decisions or start imagining the future, desiring for your dream job or marrying the love of your life, your ego takes control of your brain and your actions. What you need do in this situation is take a deep breath with your back straight, and you will feel the presence of your mind as a witness, and that will make you focus on the present.

The ego is always trying to escape the present, making the future look way better or reminding you of your past mistakes. You fail to enjoy the moments of the present and let go of the opportunities that you are offered because you are always seeking happiness in the future.

Your ego makes you wonder or worry about something that you don't have control over, the future or the past. For example, your ego judges others and wastes your energy gossiping about others. Your ego spends most of the time spending your energy wishing for things you don't have, instead of being grateful for what you already have, pushing you into a frenzy of sadness and depression. Your ego makes it hard for you to apologize for your mistakes, thus making you look like a narcissistic and an arrogant person.

The only way you can get rid of your ego is by identifying it, recognizing that it's not the real you, and that all the judgments and false identifications that seem to be coming from your mind are, in reality, coming from another entity that is controlling you and using you against your own self.

What I'm trying to say here is that life is simple. Just think about it for a second. Humans did great over the years with the things that nature provided them. Moreover, the study says that the capacity of their brains was higher than it is today. It makes sense thinking of all the distractions we are surrounded by such as scrolling, gossiping, and judging people. Don't let your ego control you. Identify it, separate it from yourself, and notice yourself growing in life.

Ego and the Soul

I believe that we, humans, are deeply connected with both our ego and our soul. We encounter them daily. Ego is the voice within us that demands too much and pulls us along the road that is extremely difficult and filled with hurdles. It robs us of the peace we deserve. On the other hand, our soul is the deep, intense, and infinitely serene place within us that knows nothing but love, compassion, empathy, and honesty. The soul is who we really are. Every human being truly deserves a chance to live the best life they can. However, our ego disrupts the process with twisted mind games. Hence, it is time to take back what belongs to us and kick ego in the face.

5 Important Rules

I suggest five crucial rules to begin experiencing the life you wish for. These rules will help you ponder over your inner world in order to let go of your ego and make the decisions about your journey through tough times of your life. Since the time I started living by these rules, I have experienced nothing but peace, passion, and meaning in my life and I hope it will do the same for you.

Connect with the World

"We cannot live only for ourselves. A thousand fibers connect us with our fellow men; and among those fibers, as

sympathetic threads, our actions run as causes, and they come back to us as effects."

-Herman Melville

Take a look around yourself, digest the perfect and unimaginable miracles of the universe, and envision your unique connection with the whole of it. Think of how lucky you are to be a part of this exotic beauty, just like all the other living creatures. We are personally connected with the entire universe at a deeper level.

Imagine how it would be if the sun does not rise one morning or if the clouds do not shower rain. We would have no food or water, we would not exist, there would be no flowers or trees, and all animals would eventually become extinct. If things, humans, and animals do not exist the way they do, we would have nothing. Thus, we are a crucial part of this eternal cycle of existence which works in harmony to create this magnificent universe.

I suggest that you connect with nature and every living thing in the world by simply relaxing your mind and becoming more outgoing. Take some time to enjoy the nature and company of other humans and, of course, some animals too. Every creature of our living cosmos deserves to be a part of the universal mystery as much as we do.

Be Grateful for Everything

"Gratitude makes sense of our past, brings peace for today, and creates a vision for tomorrow."

-Melody Beattie

Our mind and soul are always satisfied and grateful for what we have. But it is the ego that always craves for more gratification. Nothing is ever enough for it. It is simply insatiable. Its plan for you is to endlessly seek happiness and satisfaction. It urges you to wish and seek materialistic happiness which leads to an endless cycle of wanting more and more.

Look around you and you will find that there are people who may not even know what and when their next meal will be or if they will have access to clean water. Hence, always be grateful for whatever you have. Make a gratitude diary and list all the things you are grateful for. Express your gratitude openly to your loved ones. You never know how long someone is in your life.

Embrace Change

"Change will not come if we wait for some other person, or if we wait for some other time. We are the ones we've been waiting for. We are the change that we seek."

-Barack Obama

It's true when they say, change is the only constant in life and our soul knows the transience of everything in the universe. However, our ego constantly seeks control of ourselves and resists change or anything that interrupts its being. Ego's greatest game is control and it makes sure to fight this illusion till the end of time. This constant fight between the soul and the fight only causes more suffering.

If you live according to the soul, it will allow you to live graciously with the flow of life rather than constantly fighting with it. This, in exchange, gives you peace and serenity. Keep in mind that change will consistently happen in your daily life. At one point, it will happen so rapidly that you won't even have time to process it and will only approach it with acceptance and flexibility. Some changes in life may catch you by surprise, but trust me these will be the best changes in your life. Hence, embrace changes with open arms.

Live with a Big Heart

"Let us look around with a compassionate heart to feel and see the deepest joy of life."

-Debasish Mridha

Our ego often prevents us from seeing the bigger picture and keeps us busy in our head. We often feel trapped by our thoughts, worrying, obsessing, and creating more problems than they originally are. It stops us from actually connecting with nature and reaching other human beings to build meaningful relationships.

When we make a choice to truly care about others outside our potential and help them in all ways possible, we begin to unleash the power of our mind and achieve great things in the world. Hence, make a habit of helping someone daily. You will be shocked at how many opportunities await you. Just connect to the compassionate side of you and you will notice how easily you are able to communicate and relate to others. Just a simple hello, a good morning, opening the door for a stranger and listening attentively to someone can make their day and leave you feeling elevated. You will be surprised at how wonderful life is when we live it with a big heart.

Live in the Present

"Do not dwell in the past, do not dream of the future, concentrate the mind on the present moment."

-Buddha

Your ego tends to drag you in the false realities of your past and future. Understand that these DO NOT exist. There is no past and no future. The moment you currently are living in is the supreme reality. Your ego blooms in the past and the future and goes to any length to keep you imprisoned in this delusion in order to ignore its own death.

It dies when you reflect the light of the PRESENT upon it. Hence, embrace the present and you will truly know what it feels like to be genuinely alive. *Right here, Right now*, is the most important statement of our life. Our entire life is based on this unique and long-lasting moment. Throughout your day, make it a point to always remind yourself of the present moment and teach yourself to live your best life in the present. It definitely takes practice, however, being mindful of it will offer you unimaginable gifts in your life and strengthen your connection with the mind and the soul.

The Evolution from Ego to Soul

Moving forward and making your evolution from ego to soul is not that difficult and I want nothing more for you to observe the ecstasy of being guided by your splendid soul. Simply follow these five rules I have described above and you will be on the right way to live the life you truly desire. We don't realize that we humans are blessed with an infinite potential to make a huge difference here on the earth and in other's lives.

We need to take the maximum advantage of this opportunity we are given. Continue to focus and be mindful of the ego's influence on your life and how it reveals itself in your life. Just watch and become a witness of this evolution. This part of you that becomes an observer is in complete alignment with the soul. This is your sign to tap into it and allow it to spread throughout your entire existence. Try to be as mindful as possible and continue to occasionally remind yourself to come back to this strong presence. This is the presence you want in your life to guide you each moment. You will notice your ego sometimes become more demanding and taking power over your thoughts. It is okay. It is part of the transition. The goal is not to block the ego or throw it away. Instead, get to know it, become friends with it, and gently let it know that its childlike tantrums and demands are heard. However, you have decided to push them aside and live according to your mind and the soul. You will start this as a routine practice and eventually notice that it gets much easier and comes naturally as you continue repeating it.

Do It Now!

I believe now you are ready to experience the perpetual journey of your mind and soul. Trust me when I say, this is the journey of freedom and endless possibilities. When you starve your ego and feed your soul, you will experience your connection with everyone in your life growing and flourishing. Go ahead and relax in the richness of your soul and don't forget to change the world in the process.

Your Doodle Page

Starving your ego and feeding your soul can open countless opportunities in life. How do you manage to beat ego in your life? Mention below:

Chapter 5 - Perception - Present Moment

"God, grant me the serenity to accept the things I cannot change, the courage to change the things I can, and the wisdom to know the difference."

-Reinhold Niebuhr

As Reinhold puts it, by changing our perception, we can transform things or thoughts we perceived as negative and turn them into positive; it gives you power over your emotions and feelings. Being mindful about life's different experiences can help you turn the negative thoughts into positive if you just look at the bright side of life. For instance, we humans tend to ponder over our mistakes.

We think of them and feel frustrated and angry because instead of processing it as a past mistake, we carry the baggage in our present over and over again. Once I became familiar with mindfulness, I loved how I could get in the flow zone so easily. I loved the realization that I could see myself when I was not in the flow zone and so the present moment - and I could just easily with a breath bring my attention back. Everything is better in the present; everything happens naturally. Stress doesn't exist. You don't even exist. When you are in the flow zone, you lose perception of yourself, you stop thinking, and you just follow the instinct and naturally be. Another major distortion of perception is to make a mountain out of a molehill. We experience a small setback, but our overthinking makes it appear as something worse.

Overthinking and staying stuck in our past is a waste of our creativity and our potential to imagine things we don't want to happen. When you're mindful and present at the moment, you use your creativity to make unique things. You can draw, sing, write, and master playing an instrument or any other activity that brings out the best in you.

On the other hand, we often fall back on imagination and think of future events and conversations that might not even happen. This exercise brings unnecessary stress, frustration, and pressure which can deviate our minds from the big picture which is living in the present. The present moment is the only moment in your reality that you can have an effect on. The past and future are mere realities of your imagination. When you are present at the moment, you are more focused, responsive, brave, calm, and capable.

If you notice, when your mind experiences anxiety, fear, depression, and worry, you unconsciously see your mind slipping into an imaginary future or past thoughts. What we think has a big impact on how we act. Because the present is the only moment we have, we have been given more than a gift with this life, and I can't understand how people are wasting it by worrying about something that is not currently happening or something that already happened. Staying in the present helped me in my life.

When I play soccer, and someone kicks me with bad intention instead of wasting my energy thinking to hit him back, I stay in the present, focus, and score a goal. Every mistake you make is a lesson so instead of regurgitating stay present and be grateful for the lesson learned. Have trust in the process, and don't worry about the future because you have the present and every little action you take has an impact on that future.

Now, What Is a Thought?

Thoughts can represent an idea, a memory, a picture, or a song. They usually exist for a short time, unlike continuous events that last longer than usual. We are all familiar with thoughts and have no problem relating to them and speaking about them to others. From a neuroscientific point of view, thoughts still remain a mystery. They are definitely caused by brain functions, but we do not have strong proof of their existence and how they are produced. Are there some special neurons involved? Is it the way they function? Do conscious thoughts need the activation of some parts of the brain? To be honest, science has yet to prove these questions. Till then we just don't know.

The only fact we do know is that something intangible could cause us so many problems. We fail to focus on what is happening in front of us and are not able to experience life's moments and thus limit our potential for all the opportunities that we can achieve at a particular moment. Presence of mind opens up a sea of opportunities that were always there but you were too distracted in projecting yourself in the future or past to notice them. In our imaginary future, we often picture ourselves in an idealistic situation, and when the result is not as we expect it to be, we fall into a state of frustration and depression.

Mark Twain said, *"I've had a lot of catastrophes in my life, and some of them actually happened."*

We create anxiety by projecting ourselves into the situation, imagining situations, and pre-judging events before they even occur. If you've thoroughly read the previous chapters of this book, you would know that by practicing meditation and mindfulness, we perceive it to be an exception to the rule and the more we notice it, the more aware and present we become. Planning and preparation are crucial to our function and can be incorporated into present moment activities. Ask yourself if you are going to live in the illusion of your imaginative thoughts about an unreal future or past, or experience the essence of life at the present moments?

Think of a world where we witness thoughts without becoming them and experience feelings and emotions without being too overwhelmed. Some people who have nothing are happier than those who are blessed with everything and still can't get out of their pasts or worries of the future. True wealth is your perspective and the health of your brain. There are many things that may trigger your stress or the fight and flight response. These are particularly called 'stressors' and can be a situation, an event, a circumstance, or a person. For example, you're camping in a forest and a snake crosses your path.

Your reaction will determine your response. It will push you to either fight or flight at that moment. However, an imaginary stressor will also cause the activation of a response and this will happen if you unconsciously take your imagination to be a reality. Think of a student who finds it difficult to focus on their studies because the stress of their imaginary – not so real - thoughts is picturing themselves in a situation of failing the exams.

This stress makes it hard for them to focus, but if they learn how to bring their attention back in the present and consciously prepare for their exams, then there is no exam or event that can cause them stress. What is important in this situation is to see imagination for what it is - unreal.

Why Is It Difficult to Live in the Present?

Many of us suffer from a peculiar-sounding problem - an inability to inhabit the stretch of time we call 'the present.' Maybe we're on a beautiful beach on a sunny day, the sky is azure, and the palm trees slender and implausibly delicate, but most of *'us'* aren't actually here at all. We are somewhere at work or in imaginary discussion with a rival or plotting a new business. Maybe we're physically at the birthday of a child.

It's hugely significant for them and we love them dearly, but we are elsewhere. Our body is rooted in the now, but our minds are skipping to points in both the future and in the past. What is it that makes the present, especially the nicer moments of the present so difficult to experience properly? And why, conversely, can so many events feel easier to enjoy, appreciate, and perceive, when they are firmly over? One benefit of the past is that it is a dramatically foreshortened edited version of the present.

Even the best days of our lives contain a range of dull and uncomfortable moments. But in memory, like skilled editors of hours of raw and often uninspired footage, we hold on to the most consequential moments, and therefore construct sequences that feel a great deal more meaningful and interesting than the settings that generated them.

Hours of mediocrity can be reduced to five or six perfect images. Nostalgia is the present enhanced by an editing machine.Much of what ruins the present is sheer anxiety. The present always contains an enormous number of possibilities, some hugely gruesome, which we are constantly aware of in the background. Anything could happen theoretically - an earthquake, an aneur ysm, a rejection which gives rise to the non-specific anxiety that trails most of us around all the time, and a simple dread at the unknowingness of what is to come. But then, of course, only a very limited range of awful things do ever come to pass and we forget the anxiety at once, or rather shift it to the new present. So when we remember an event, what we leave out of it is how much of that event we actually spent anticipating an appalling future that never came. Our bodies further contribute to our distraction from the present.

They have their own moods and itineraries. They may feel tired and timid at just the moment when the landscape around us demands grandeur and confidence. But these dissonant moods also get edited out of memory. We remember the view over the ocean longer than the slight queasiness which turned us in on ourselves at the time.

Our minds are cavernous, chaotic places. So much runs through them that has little to do with what is right in front of our eyes. We end up seeming ungrateful to where we are. Someone tells us an important story, not with any evil motive. And just from the difficulty of having to manage the entity called *I*, we digest some regret or other instead. We are at a beautiful location, but we can barely take in the vegetation and the extraordinary views, so fixated are we on an event that will only occur in six months' time.

We need to be prepared for the weird way in which we align with the world and not berate ourselves unduly for our difficulties in doing justice to where our bodies and minds happen to be. We should be ready for this disloyalty from other people too, at moments when they look strangely worried at a party. They too may be experiencing some of the major difficulties of being in the present. Like us, they'll probably enjoy our encounter with us so much more when the present has safely given way to memory.

Ways to Live in the Present

"Do not dwell in the past, do not dream of the future, concentrate the mind on the present moment."

-Buddha

In reality, there is only one time and place you can be and have control over. That is the present moment. But many of us experience a lot of our regular days lost in the memories of the past, reliving a sunny afternoon, or maybe repeating an old argument or negative thoughts in our head over and over again. We get lost in the events of the future - most probably wishful thinking, or feeding the demons in our minds making them scarier and too dangerous to live in. Our thoughts may split between several different tasks and things we need to focus on. If you find yourself spending a lot of your everyday moments and time in the past or the future, or you are having difficulty focusing on tasks that need your full attention and are having a negative effect on your life, then maybe you need to learn to live in the present moment. Here's what I've been implementing throughout my life and I suggest that you do the same. Just a few simple techniques and you'll be a pro at enjoying your present.

Work on a Single Task

Many others including me often talk about how important single-tasking is to get your work done efficiently. I realize that it becomes a lot easier for me to live in the present throughout the day If I just single-task everything I do.

This means not to open several tabs when I'm browsing the internet, but to be fully engaged with one task I am doing online. It also means not to use my cell phone or laptop as I watch the television, or to simply avoid using electronic devices when engaging in a conversation with someone.

Give your day a good start and set the pace for it by doing one thing at a time starting from the time you wake up and go to bed by the end of the day. If you have to multitask, then set some time apart for it during the day. Make sure it's not more than an hour.

Do It Gradually

When you wake up in the morning and go about doing your first task of the day, do it gradually. There is no need to speed things up. Do your present task and the next few at a relaxed and calm speed. It will supposedly not take that much of your time than if you did it quickly.

You will be able to stay more present and focused on each thing individually and also find joy in the simplest tasks. You will realize that the tasks you once dreaded doing are now more fun and easier.

Try this technique once instead of speeding things up and then messing them and getting stuck in worries or loops of what might happen today or tomorrow before you even eat your breakfast. As you get into the habit of doing things slowly, you will realize a unique calmness and peace in doing the most difficult tasks also.

Say to Yourself: Now I Am...

As I take on any task, I simply whisper to myself: Now I am _____. For instance, if I am eating food, I tell myself: Now I am eating my food. It might sound a little absurd in the beginning but once you get the hang of it, you will realize how important it is when doing tasks, where it is easy to get distracted into the past or future.

You could exercise this habit when you're brushing your teeth or hair, when you're taking a walk down the road, and when you're reading a book or doing homework. You don't have to say it to yourself all the time but a few times throughout the day will be just fine.

Limit What You Give Access to in Your Head

Checking your Facebook or other social media accounts first thing in the morning has had an adverse effect on your mind. I have realized that this specific activity puts more irrelevant thoughts in my mind that are not supposed to be there in the first place at all. This makes it harder for you to concentrate on the important tasks, to stay present, and not get distracted by negative thoughts. So be kind to yourself and try not to check anything on your phone for the first 20 minutes of waking up. You can definitely check them throughout the day, but I suggest that you limit that use too. Once you start limiting your social media use, you will notice your days becoming lighter, brighter, and simpler. You will not only be more present but also get more things done throughout the day.

Go with the Flow to Make the Most Out of a Situation

Psychologists say the best way of completely living in your present moment is the absorption of flow. Flow arises when you are so involved in your tasks that you lose track of time, your surroundings, and everything else around you. But that raises an interesting question: how can I be living at the moment when I'm unaware of my surroundings?

See, the depth of involvement absorbs your power, keeping you attentive and focused that distractions cannot enter your mind. You focus so passionately that you're unaware of how fast time passes by. Hours seem minutes when you're engrossed in an intriguing task.

Flow is an abstract state, just like romance or sleep. You can't push yourself into it. All you can do is set the scene, creating an optimal situation for it to happen. To get into the flow of doing things naturally, you first need to set goals that are challenging but not impossible - something you have to fetch resources for and push yourself to achieve it. The goals you set should match your level of ability - not so difficult that you feel drained and stressed out in achieving them. Your goals need to be clearly defined so that you are familiar with your next step, whether it's playing the next chord or finding the next foothold while climbing a hill, or turning a page when reading a book.

As your focus narrows, you will observe self-consciousness evaporating. You will feel your awareness merging with the actions you are performing. You will feel a sense of hold over the situation. This exercise is so rewarding that although the task is hard, the action feels easy.

Know That There Are Things You May Not Know

I'm sure you've probably experienced driving on a deserted street and suddenly realized you have no idea of the previous fifteen minutes. You're not sure if you missed the exit or took a wrong turn. You feel completely zoned out. Or maybe the same thing happened when you were reading a book: *"I think I just read the page, but I have no idea what it was about."*

Harvard Professor Ellen Langer calls these autopilot moments *mindfulness*. These are times when we are so lost in our thought that we're completely unaware of our present situation. As a result, life moves without you on board. The easiest way to avoid these blackouts is to make a habit of noticing new things in every situation you are. This process creates active engagement with your present reality and releases a series of other benefits along the way. Observing and keeping track of new things puts you thoughtfully in the present moment.

We automatically become mindful and present because when we think we already know something, we stop paying attention to it. We go about living our day casually because we've been through the same road many times before. But if you truly open your eyes and set yourself up to notice something different and new in a day, you will realize how everything is completely different - the patterns of sunlight on the buildings, the wrinkles on people's faces, the sounds of the birds, or as simple as the feelings you experience along the day. Noticing instills each moment with a new and fresh quality. This state is also known as 'beginner's mind'.

Don't Do Anything, Just Sit – For Now

Continuously living in a state of mindfulness takes effort. But the process itself is effortless and easy. Mindfulness is the only conscious activity that does not force you to improve or change yourself. It is simply about realizing where you are at that moment. You can enter the state of mindfulness at any moment of the day by just paying attention to your surroundings. In fact, you can do it right now while reading this book.

What is happening around you now? How present are you? Think of yourself as a witness and just observe the current moment. What do you hear, smell, or see? It doesn't matter if it feels pleasant or unpleasant, good or bad, or if it stinks – you let it be because it's what's present at the moment. You don't have to judge the situation, simply take it in, and engross yourself in it. If you feel your mind is tired of noticing or distracting, just repeat to yourself: Now, Now, Now.

It's important to know that mindfulness is not a goal, because, my friend, you make goals for the future and mindfulness is in the present. As you inhale your next breath, focus on the rise and fall of your chest, the stream of warm air passing through your nostrils, and the heaviness in your lungs. If you're aware of this feeling right now as you're reading this book, congratulations, because you're living in the present moment. Do not feel anxious about the future. Nothing will happen next. There is no other destination. This is the only present. And you are already here.

Your Doodle Page

Anxiety about the future does not help. Strive to live in the present. How do you challenge to live in the present in life? Write your personal struggle below:

Chapter 6 - Move!

"You can motivate by fear, and you can motivate by reward. But both those methods are only temporary. The only lasting thing is self-motivation."

-Homer Rice

Right now, you're probably sitting down to read this book. Staying seated for a few minutes to read it is probably okay. However, the longer you stay fixed in one place, the more stressed your body becomes. Your body sits there counting the seconds until you stand up and move or take it out for a walk. That may sound absurd. Our bodies love to be seated, right?

Nowadays, our routine makes us sit much more than we move, and our bodies aren't built for such an inactive existence. In fact, just the contrary is true. The human body is built to move, and we can see proof of that in the way it is designed. Inside our body are over 360 joints and about 700 skeletal muscles that allow relaxed, fluid motions. Our body's distinctive physical assembly gives us the ability to stand up straight against the pull of gravity.

Our blood depends on us to move around frequently for it to circulate properly. Our brain cells benefit from movement, and our skin is flexible, meaning it molds to our movements. So if every part of the body is ready and waiting for us to move, what will happen when we don't? Let's begin with the backbone of the problem, literally. Our spine is a long structure made of bones and the cartilage disks located between them. Joints, muscles, and ligaments that are devoted to the bones hold it all together.

A common way of sitting is with an arched back and drooping shoulders, a position that puts uneven weight on our spine. Over time, this leads to wear and tear in our spinal disks, overburdens some ligaments and joints, and puts pressure on muscles that stretch to accommodate our back's arched position.

This stooped shape shrinks our chest cavity while we are seated, meaning our lungs have less space to inflate into when we breathe. That is a problem because it briefly limits the amount of oxygen that fills our lungs and sieves into our blood. Around the skeleton are the muscles, nerves, arteries, and veins that form the body's soft tissue deposits. The very act of sitting squeezes coerces and compresses, and these more gentle tissues feel the force.

Have you ever faced unresponsiveness and inflammation in your limbs when you sit? In areas that are the more trampled, your nerves, arteries, and veins can become choked, which restricts nerve signaling and causing the unresponsiveness, and decreases blood flow in our limbs causing them to swell. Sitting for longer periods temporarily neutralizes lipoprotein lipase, a unique enzyme in the walls of blood capillaries that disintegrates fats in the blood, so when we sit, we're not burning fat practically as well as when we move around.

What impact does all of this stillness have on the brain? Most of the time, we perhaps sit down to use our brain, but oddly, prolonged periods of sitting actually run opposite to this goal. Being immobile reduces blood flow and the volume of oxygen entering our bloodstream through our lungs. Our brain needs both of these things to remain active, so our focus level most likely declines as our brain activities are reduced. Unfortunately, the hostile effects of being seated don't occur for the short term. Recent studies have discovered that sitting for long periods is related to some types of cancer and heart disease and can also add to diabetes, kidney, and liver complications.

In fact, researchers have figured out that internationally, idleness causes about nine percent of impulsive deaths a year. That's around five million people. So it seems like such a bland habit can actually affect our health. Fortunately, the answers to this growing threat are humble and intuitive. When you have no choice but to sit, try swapping the hunch for a straighter spine, and when you don't have to be restricted to your seat, try to move around much more, maybe by setting a reminder to yourself to get up every half hour. Generally, just appreciate that bodies are made for motion, not for immobility. Treat your body to a walk. It'll thank you in the future.

Not just the spine, but when we are sitting, all our muscles and joints feel the pressure. They are worn out and are prone to degeneration earlier than they usually do. The more we sit, the faster our body gets tired and loses its elasticity. This elasticity can be gained back through movement of any kind, be it walking, sports, jogging, or simply exercising for at least 20 minutes a day. Research states that exercise improves our memory and cognition. A study showed that just 20 minutes of walking enhanced a person's long-term memory by about 10 percent.

Exercise is the most evolutionary movement our body can experience for two essential reasons.

- It has instant effects on our brain. A single workout immediately escalates the level of neurotransmitters like dopamine, serotonin, and noradrenaline in our brain. These precursors significantly improve our mood right after the workout. A single workout can surge our ability to shift and focus attention. That focus on upgrading lingers for at least two hours. Finally, research has shown that a single workout expands our reaction time which means that you are going to be faster at grabbing that cup of Starbucks that drops off the counter. However, these instant effects are temporary. You mainly have to change your exercise routine and intensify your cardiorespiratory function to get the long-lasting effects. These effects are long-lasting because the exercise actually alters the brain's anatomy, make-up, and function. My favorite brain area is the hippocampus. The exercise actually yields brand new brain cells that increase its volume, as well as improve your long-term memory.

- Secondly, the most common discovery in neuroscience research, observing the long-term exercise, is enriched attention function reliant on your prefrontal cortex. You do not only get better focus and attention but also the capacity of hippocampus surges. Finally, you not only get instant effects of mood with exercise but those also last for a long time. The most revolutionary thing that exercise does is protect your brain. Here you can perceive the brain as a muscle. The more you work out, the bigger and stronger your hippocampus and prefrontal cortex gets. Why is that important? Because the prefrontal cortex and the hippocampus are the two main areas that are most vulnerable to neurodegenerative diseases and typical cognitive decline in aging. So with improved exercise over your lifetime, you're not going to cure Dementia or Alzheimer's disease, but what you're going to do is you're going to build the strongest, biggest hippocampus and prefrontal cortex, so it takes longer for these diseases to actually have an impact on you. Hence, you can think of exercise as an amplified 401k for your brain. It's even better since it's free.

For this to happen, I recommend a walk after meals, so it helps with digestion and activates your brain. A 30-minute exercise daily allows blood to flow regularly and not get locked into your legs. I personally got the best feeling ever when I discovered the power of walking barefoot on the grass or sand. I grew up in Milan, a big industrial city where unfortunately I didn't have access to the nature that I now do. I was lucky that I played soccer 90 percent of my time, but now that I know the power of walking barefoot around nature, my whole life has changed. I don't see how people don't realize that they are spending so much time seated or not moving.

Let's reassume what an average person who does a 9-5 job does: wake up after lying in bed for 8 hours, take a car to work maybe for an hour, sit at work for 8 hours, go back home after an hour seated in public transport or car, then eat while still seated and then sleep. In all this time, he might sometimes get to include 30 minutes of exercise, two or three days a week. That really should be the opposite. You should move ALL THE TIME and ONLY rest when you actually need to rest. As humans, we have evolved through walking everywhere to find food and a better climate. How did we not realize this? Funny story: after I spent my whole year in

Melbourne I changed quite radically as a person, so when I got back in Milan for a holiday to see my family I could see they noticed the change in many different ways. A funny one was when they look at me like I was crazy when I told my friends that after a night out I was going to have a walk because I needed to think about a couple of things. They were making fun of me for the fact that I was taking walks and talking about mediation they were looking at me weirdly, but they also appreciated the change, and now they are embracing it as well.

A different study states that daily exercise helps fight depression. That is only because our brain stimulates substances such as endorphins, serotonin, dopamine that are also known as the feel-good hormones. Creativity also gets stimulated by physical exercise. Stanford University research has shown that a 30-minute walk every day increases creativity by up to 60%.

Swedish researchers have proven that exercise reduces stress and depression as it turns out that our muscles have a higher level of an enzyme that helps metabolize - a stress chemical called Kynurenine.

Exercise and Depression

"If you can believe it, the mind can achieve it."

-Ronnie Lott

When we exercise, our body discharges chemicals called endorphins. These endorphins interact with the receptors in our brain that reduce our perception of pain. Endorphins are also responsible for positive feelings in the body, similar to that of morphine. For instance, the feeling that follows a good exercise session is described as *ecstatic*. This feeling, known as *runner's drug*, can be supplemented by a positive and energizing view on life.

Acupuncture, an ancient Chinese healthcare system, aims to prevent and cure specific diseases and conditions by sticking very fine, solid needles into points of the body. It is also a way to stimulate pain suppressing endorphins in the body. Endorphins act as painkillers, which means they diminish pain. They also act as sedatives. They are produced in our brain, spinal cord, and many other parts of our body, in reaction to neurotransmitters. The receptors that endorphins are attached to are the same ones that bind to some pain medicines.

However, unlike morphine, the activation of these receptors by the body's endorphins does not lead to addiction and helps with combating depression.

Regular exercise has been proven to:

- Reduce stress
- Fight anxiety and depression
- Boost self-esteem
- Improve sleep patterns
- Strengthen heart
- Elevate energy level
- Reduce blood pressure
- Improve muscle tone
- Strengthen bones
- Reduce body fat
- Keep you healthy and fit

Since strong support is necessary for those suffering from depression, joining a group exercise class can be advantageous. In doing so, you will benefit from both physical activity and emotional support. The advantages of exercise are numerous. It is important to see how each neurotransmitter affects our brain when we move and exercise.

Dopamine

Dopamine is an exceptionally famous neurotransmitter released from physical movement. This chemical is one of the crucial power drivers for all work of our brain. Without dopamine, we would act quite un-human, because it is the vital force behind most of our actions and social relationships. It is a chemical that our body releases naturally and especially after exercise.

It is the element responsible for our dreams and biggest secrets. In short, dopamine means lust, love, adultery, motivation, focus, femininity, learning, and addiction. It is also known as the reward molecule since it is responsible for reward-driven behavior. Every time you set a goal and you achieve it, your brain gets a kick of dopamine.

This is why it is recommended to maintain a to-do list and cross every activity done because it is the most effective way to boost our happiness. It is the main chemical in our brain that controls how we recognize or experience pleasure. During exercise or any other pleasurable moment, this neurotransmitter causes a person to pursue out a desirable activity over and over again, which is why we feel the need to hit the gym again and again.

Consuming food with a high level of sugar or having intercourse regularly and working out are some triggers that release dopamine in the brain. This is the reason it is suggested to move around often and engage in motivating activities.

Besides being the vital motivator, an endless supply of dopamine in our body can:

- Help lose weight
- Improve memory
- Prevent self-harm
- Fight depression
- Resist impulsive behavior
- Reduce chances of Parkinson's disease

"Movement is a medicine for creating change in a person's physical, emotional, and mental states."

-Carol Welch

Oxytocin

Oxytocin is also known as the *bonding molecule* or the *love hormone* linked to the skin-to-skin contact, affection, and lovemaking. Did you ever think there would be science behind a hug? Well, here you go. Research shows that hugs boost our happiness through the stimulation of oxytocin in the brain. This is one of the main reasons we get addicted to a person in a relationship or adopt a pet. When we feel we need love, our brain tries different ways to stimulate this hormone to improve our mood. Studies reveal that couples who hug more and more are likely to stay together for longer periods. A good hug lasts for 20 seconds.

However, there are other activities too that stimulate the release of oxytocin, such as exercise. Research conducted in 2007 at the Society of Neuroscience concluded that oxytocin's effects are more apparent under tense situations. In the study, people suffering from anxiety, stress, and depression were injected with the hormone that instantly suppressed the negative emotions.

Considering its ability to reduce social obstacles, induce feelings of optimism, increase self-esteem, and build love, oxytocin is progressively observed as a hormone that helps overcome fears. Research shows that it may be useful in handling shyness or helping people with social anxiety and mood disorder. Additionally, it is considered a way of helping people to treat autism, as it is included in one of the common social communication disorders.

Serotonin

Serotonin is an important brain substance that helps transfer messages throughout the nervous system. This chemical executes many functions including controlling mood, appetite, and sleep patterns. Exercise and eating certain foods increase serotonin levels in the body. The National Institute of Health and Clinical Excellence of the U.K. discloses that exercise increases brain serotonin level. A systematic exercise program increases the level of tryptophan (an acid that produces serotonin). Serotonin is also known as the confidence molecule that gets stimulated every time you win a challenge or get rewarded.

It is the feeling of accomplishment when you challenge yourself and say to yourself, *"I did it!"* It significantly increases your self-esteem. Though many other chemicals take part in the body to influence our mood, serotonin is one of the most important hormones that control our mood. External factors such as sunlight, diet, and exercise are major stimulators. This chemical also decreases heart diseases such as heart attacks and strokes. It is a natural antidepressant that significantly glows the skin. Serotonin also helps to get rid of free radical cells. It yields antioxidants in the body to fight free radicals that are known for promoting aging.

Deficiency of serotonin can cause disrupted sleep patterns. This can be treated by consuming supplements to boost the serotonin level in the body and thus eradicate the problem. Low amount of serotonin in the body can also lead to binging. The affected person is unable to control their eating habit and is thus affected by obesity and increased level of depression and anxiety.

GABA

Researchers from the University of California at Davis observed that exercise increases levels of two common neurotransmitters – glutamate and gamma-aminobutyric acid (GABA) that are responsible for delivering chemical messages between neurons within the brain. GABA is the main inhibitory source. Its role is to decrease the movement of neurons throughout the nervous system.

In humans, GABA is also accountable for the regulation of muscle tone. This is only found in individuals who exercise often and keep their bodies in constant motion. It plays an active role in the smooth functioning of the body's immune and endocrine system, as well as modifying appetite and metabolism. There is also noteworthy research on GABA's role in the gut and stomach functions, where it works to support flexibility, curb inflammation, and control the hormone activity. It is also presented as a complement to treat high blood pressure, stress, anxiety, and sleep. It is a crucial provider of the body's overall mental and physical homeostasis or movement.

Deficiency of GABA in the body can lead to:

- Anxiety
- Chronic stress
- Depression
- Memory problems
- Difficulty in concentration
- Muscle pain
- Headache
- Insomnia and sleep problems

These molecules are produced in large quantity during high-intensity training as strength and cardio exercise. GABA, also known as the anti-anxiety molecule, creates a sense of calmness in humans. Activities such as yoga, meditation, and writing a diary of your thoughts are well-known to stimulate this molecule.

Neuroplasticity

Neuroplasticity is the brain's incredible ability to adjust to new experiences. It denotes the biological changes in the brain that happen as a result of our association with the environment. From the time the brain starts to develop in the uterus till the day we die, the association between the cells in the brain rearranges in response to our changing needs. This vigorous process allows us to continuously change and adapt.

It is the basis of most of our cognitive and physical rehabilitation activities. One of these rehabilitation practices comprises exercise being on top of the list. Both neuroplasticity and exercise help us build new muscles in our brain and body. Both of these processes make us stronger internally and externally. Neuroplasticity is a process in itself, but exercise is a stimulator that simply boosts its functions and enhances its benefits.

Neuroplasticity has proven that we can change our brain. Our brain is a muscle. We need to exercise regularly. Try something different. Try something new. Stay curious. Every time we experience something *new*, our brain gets stimulated and improved. The best way to enhance the capacity of our brain is to explore, experiment, and try new things to maximize our brainpower usage.

"Exercise to stimulate, not to annihilate. The world wasn't formed in a day, and neither were we. Set small goals and build upon them."

-Lee Haney

Our body needs to move, whether as a part of a dynamic lifestyle or a rigorous exercise program. Movement is connected to every function and process in the body. External movements of the body are reliant on joints and muscles and actions that work them constantly. Movement is important for every phase of health, whether it's exercise, a walk, yoga, or as simple as indulging in aerobics.

At the very basic, human beings are simply energies in motion. It is hard to identify the difference between moving and simply existing. The more stationary your life is, the more significant it is to voluntarily move or participate in activities that stimulate any kind of movement. I ask myself why? I think it is very important to have a clear purpose in life and mine now is to help other people getting out of that dark room. I was living in a box mental prison until knowing this that changed my life, that's why I believe writing is so important because it helps you keep your thoughts and purpose clear to you and bring it into awareness. The way of life is by far the most important factor that controls the type, amount, and occurrence of movement that a person engrosses in. Make sure you make it worthwhile and move enough to embrace its benefits. Always remember, movement of the body leads to a healthy and happy lifestyle that is important to the well-being of all humans.

Your Doodle Page

Staying still has never won anyone anything. Express, in your words, how you intend on to stay active in life:

Chapter 7 - Our Brain

"Everything we do, every thought we've ever had, is produced by the human brain. But exactly how it operates remains one of the biggest unsolved mysteries, and it seems the more we probe its secrets, the more surprises we find."

-Neil deGrasse Tyson

Some 1800 years ago, a German physician Franz Joseph Gall spent most of his time running his fingers through his own hair and over the scalp of strangers. He was neither a male masseuse nor a hairdresser, nor a big fan of strangers' heads. He was a phrenologist. He supposed that a person's personality was connected to their skull's anatomy and that its bumps and folds signaled traits of their character.

Surprisingly, this idea prevailed and was widely practiced for years. Soon, he became a celebrity during his time. However, phrenology was rejected as a cult pseudoscience because it led to the conclusion that our cranial structure tells us nothing about what's happening inside the brain. On the other hand, Gall was trying to figure out something big, something that we had no idea of.

His proposition was that different parts of the brain control certain aspects of our behavior. Like we discussed in the previous chapter, there is a strong connection between biological activity and psychological action. Additionally, the interaction of chemicals like neurotransmitters and hormones is linked to a few parts of the brain having precise functions such as vision, movement, memory, speech, and even facial expressions. This is the connection between the brain - walnut-shaped structure between the ears - and the mind - the thing that comprises ourselves, our consciousness, our behaviors, our decisions, our memories, and our actions.

Some scientists believe that *the mind is what the brain does*. So, one of the intriguing questions is, *"How do our brains' functions connect to the behavior of the mind?"* Honestly, you can never know the answer to this until you get to know the brain. You might be familiar with your nervous system on some basic level, *"The brain bone is attached to the spinal cord, and the spinal cord is attached to the motoneuron bone."*

The Curious Case of Phineas Gage

In 1848, a railroad construction worker, Phineas Gage was working on the railroad. He was cramming gunpowder into a stubborn hole using an iron rod, when the gunpowder exploded. The ignition caused the rod to fire like a bullet up through his left cheek and out of the top of his head. You know there is a brain between those two places. Shockingly, he stood up after the calamity, walked over to his carriage, and described to others what had happened.

They drove him back to his house. Throughout this time he was conscious. A doctor came to observe Phineas and denied to believe that a rod had passed through his head. Until Phineas began coughing and a part of the brain that the doctor described as a cupful fell out of his head, the doctor had to accept what exactly had happened. After a few months of recovering, Phineas started moving around like he used to.

However, his friends complained that he was no longer like himself. While the previous Phineas was well-mannered and soft-spoken, now he had become rude, mean-spirited, and discourteous. People started to label him as *'No longer Gage.'* Phineas left America, the scientific institution lost contact with him, and 12 years later, after a number of seizures, he passed away at the age of 36. Phineas is an excellent example of how physical and biological aspects can be mirrored in psychological ways. He is also a brilliant example of how specific studies are not valuable, mainly since we have very little information on what he was actually like before the tragedy occurred. It is possible that he continued to recover and lived the rest of his life as a satisfied and productive man.

Introduction to psychology books often paints the picture of Phineas so we can have a basic and clear example of the moment when doctors realized that messing with the brain meant messing with the mind. However, it is much more complex, and Phineas was an actual, real-life person.

You might have heard that we only use about 10 percent of our brain. If that is true, Phineas would use a section of his and he would be just fine. However, in reality, brain scans show that nearly every part of the brain lights up during even simple tasks like walking and eating. Not only that, but the brain requires 20 percent of all the body's energy. It makes no sense to throw much energy away at something that is only slightly active.

Components of Our Brain

As humans, our competencies have developed in part from our brain anatomy. We are actually able to reflect on our evolutionary history as we come to appreciate these frameworks. Animals that are less complex have simpler brains designed for basic functioning and survival - rest, breathe, and eat. Meanwhile, more complex animals like mammals possess brains that feel, remember, reason, and predict.

These animals do not have unique systems. They have new brain systems developed upon old brain systems. Our brain is similar to a set of Russian nesting dolls. The outermost wooden doll is the newest, most well-designed, and most complex. But as you dig deeper, the dolls become older, smaller, simpler, and more basic. The innermost wooden doll is the oldest, most generic. It is like a vestige in your head.

The innermost core of the brain sometimes refers to the 'old brain' and performs as much as it did for our historical ancestors. It is secured by the brainstem, the most primeval and central core of the brain where the spinal brain enters the skull. Above it, at the bottom of the skull, is the medulla. Here, old brain's functions occur spontaneously without any mindful effort - the thumping of the heart, the breathing of the lungs, the cleaning of the blood vessels, etc. The pons helps coordinate movement. Beyond the pons, at the top of the brainstem, is the thalamus, a pair of oval-shaped structures that accept sensory information related to seeing, hearing, tasting, and touching. The reticular development is a finger-shaped nerve network inside the brainstem that is fundamental for arousal, which is not certain what you feel upon seeing a particularly nice-looking person, yet indicates to the things like sleeping, walking, and pain perception - other vital functions.

The baseball-sized cerebellum or 'small brain' billows from the bottom of the brainstem and accounts for non-verbal learning and memory, awareness of time, and controlling emotions. It controls voluntary movements like your exotic dance moves.

It also gets compromised easily under the effect of alcohol. Hence, the old brain system keeps our body's general functions working smoothly - the kind of stuff any animal requires. This is pretty much where the brain halts for reptiles. For greater functions, we move to the limbic system. This comprises the amygdala, hypothalamus, and hippocampus — kind of a border region of the brain, splitting the old brain and the newer, higher cerebral areas. The amygdala is made up of two bean-sized bunches of neurons and accounts for memory association as well as both our greatest fear and fieriest aggression. The hypothalamus keeps our whole body stable, modifying body temperatures, circadian rhythms, and hunger. It also aids in the endocrine system, especially the pituitary gland. We should be grateful to our hypothalamus for enabling us to feel pleasure and reward.

The last part of the limbic system is the hippocampus, central to learning and memory. If that is damaged or faces trauma, a person may lose their ability to preserve new facts and memories. Beyond all of this is the most advanced substance that you think about when you think of the brain – the gray matter.

The two hemispheres of our cerebrum make about 85 percent of our brain's weight and supervise our ability to think, speak, and perceive. The left and right hemispheres rule and control different functions, giving a divided brain, attached by a structure called the corpus callosum. For example, language development is primarily controlled by the left hemisphere, while certain unique functions are controlled by the right one.

However, this has nothing to do with the handedness or people having dominant sides of their brain being more logical or creative – that's part of what we call *pop psychology*. This is a personality disorder which journalists and psychologists use showing aesthetically detailed, powerfully connected intricacies of our brain to sell newspapers or support previously held beliefs. Lastly, covering the left and right hemispheres, we have the cerebral cortex, a thin layer of over twenty billion interrelated neurons. Let's not forget the unrewarded heroes of our nervous system - the billions of non-neuron glial cells, which provide a network of support that surrounds, protects, and nourishes the cerebral neurons.

You must have seen enough brain diagrams to know that the cerebral cortex's left and right sides are further divided into four lobes: the frontal, parietal, occipital, and temporal, all parted by protruding folds or fissures. Every lobe does have its own set of responsibilities and would have made Gall proud. The frontal lobes, just after our forehead, participate in speaking, planning, judging, thinking, and as the story of Phineas reminds us, traits of personality. The parietal lobes collect and process our senses of touch and body position.

At the back of our head, the occipital lobes receive information related to sight. The temporal lobes, just above our ears, process sound, including speech comprehension. Remember that each hemisphere regulates the opposite side of the body, so our left temporal lobe processes sound heard through our right ear. Within these lobes, there are still more regions that have specific functions. Our motor-cortex at the front of frontal lobes, for instance, controls voluntary movements and sends messages from the brain out to the body like *'pet that cat'* or *'lift that leg,'* while your somatosensory cortex right behind it processes incoming sensations like *Oooh, that pillow is so soft!* Or *Gah! The cup is so warm.*

The remaining of our gray matter is made up of connected areas that are related to higher cerebral functions like remembering, thinking, learning, and speaking. The problem about connected areas is that unlike your sensory or motor cortex, you cannot just poke one and create a proper response. Connected areas are more delicate. They deal with things like understanding and assimilating sensory input and linking up with memories. They succeed throughout all four lobes, so brain damage to different areas causes different results.

An injury to a particular part of the temporal lobe may abolish a person's ability to recognize faces. Traumatic memories or abnormal hormones can intensely affect our behavior and emotions, all of which remind us how essentially biology and psychology are entangled.

Neuroplasticity

One of the most important findings of the study of neurons is the fact that our brain constantly changes in response to what we pay attention to. We discover that the billions of nerve cells (neurons) are able to create new connections and pathways and also produce new neurons in certain areas of the brain. We think that our brain was largely formed in our mother's womb and during the first few years of our life and then the remaining part of our brain became fixed with slow degeneration as we age.

However, research shows what we pay attention to and practice repeatedly grows stronger in our brain. Think of your brain as a muscle that gets stronger and more capable as it is used. This discovery was made possible, thanks to our brain imaging technology such as the electroencephalogram (EEG) and functional magnetic resonance imaging (fMRI) that show how the brain is structured and how it functions.

For example, when people practice piano over a certain period of time, new neuron connections are created in certain areas of the brain associated with finger-like movements, and the ability to differentiate among different musical tones grows stronger. What is interesting is the fact that imaging oneself doing an activity without physically doing it produces the same changes. A study was conducted by taking two different groups of people and analyzing the imaging of the area of the brain. The results of the group that was just imaging them playing the piano (without touching the keyboard) activated the same area of the brain of the group that was actually practicing it.

When every aspect of the human brain is working together in harmony, we are blessed with the symphony of multi-sensory experiences and sensations. We can understand language and communicate extraordinarily complicated ideas with each other. We can appreciate the beauty of nature and discover what it feels like to find meaning in our lives. The whole brain when functioning correctly is a phenomenal death, coordinating 20 billion bits of information every second and mapping a three-dimensional projection of the world in an outbreak of insight and deeply personal experiences.

NICOLÓ DI LEO LANZA

The human brain is capable of producing anything from a profound transcendental meditative experience to being triggered into a senseless bit of rage, fear, or depression. What makes our brains react the way they do? Is there a reliable way to condition our brain for better experiences? At birth, the human brain is a flood of superfluous connections with almost every part of the brain connected to every other part of the brain during the first two years of life.

The human brain undergoes the first major stage of the lifelong process of synaptic pruning. It is the process of synapse elimination that occurs in a developing brain that detaches unnecessary connections. The selection of the pruned connections probably uses it or loses it principally for neurons that are wired together.

This means synapses that are frequently used have strong connections while the rarely used two synapses are eliminated. Pruning is influenced by many environmental factors and is widely thought to represent learning. The developing brain sheds unnecessary connections and empowers the connections. The brain creates a specific and mature circuitry that is primed for handling the complexities of daily life.

The associations formed at childhood are thought to be replaced by more complex structures that are better suited for adulthood. Furthermore, synaptic pruning is also associated with neural Darwinism. When a herd of bison is hunted, the slowest bison at the back of the herd is most likely to die. This process of thinning the herd leaves the herd faster and more efficient. Likewise, cutting off the weakest, most unused connections leads the whole brain more efficient. The unnecessary connection in the brain is integral to energy conservation. The adult human brain consumes an enormous amount of energy - about 25% of all calories.

Even though it only comprises about 2% of total body weight, that's nothing during infancy and childhood. The brain has been shown to use between 44 percent and 87 percent of the total energy consumed in the resting body. This incredible amount of energy allocation is why humans spend almost twice as long in childhood and adolescence than our primate cousins, known as the extensive tissue hypothesis. Researchers have found that when the brain demands lots of energies, body growth slows but synaptic pruning doesn't stop.

In adulthood, the human brain continues to shed and strengthen connections throughout our entire life - a process in which we can actively play a part. Researching this phenomenon of continual synaptic pruning in the matured human brain has led to a very exciting field of study called *neuroplasticity*. You may wonder why this field of study is important to you. Well, neuroplasticity implies that you have the ability to change your brain.

Just imagine that your brain is currently processing an untold amount of data, but you are only aware of a tiny fraction of it. Rewiring your brain to process incoming data in new ways is the ultimate key to changing your life for the better. Destroying bad neural connections and strengthening empowering ones is the answer to opening yourself up to new experiences and novel states of consciousness.

How can we do that? By simply embracing the two game-changing principles of neuroplasticity: neurons that fire together wire together, and if you don't use it, you lose it. We all have a say in what thoughts we choose to think and what emotions we give our attention to. A simple change in our beliefs can have a profound impact on how our brain processes data on top of our thoughts, emotions, and beliefs. We are constantly writing the blueprints of our neural circuitry through our daily routines and rituals. Just imagine what neural connections you will change if you spend your work commute in a state of gratitude instead of a fit of anger and road rage. There are absolutely no known limits to how much you can affect the way your brains are wired up. Hence, become the subject of your own life experiment, limit time spent endorsing negative thoughts, and maximize the volume of positive ones. Develop and explore empowering emotional states and stay aware of how your feelings affect. The way you process reality challenges your beliefs and replaces any limiting concepts with new values that support your growth and evaluate your daily routines.

Don't forget to take actions to eliminate any destructive or distracting behaviors. Start introducing liberating rituals such as meditation in your life. Pursue new experiences, free yourself from your past attachments and perceptions, and use your imagination to access your highest potential. Maximize the capacity of your five senses and go beyond the limits of your ordinary mind. The gift of a living human brain is a present that defies all comprehensions. Access the power of neuroplasticity and change your brain to change your life.

Prefrontal Cortex

The prefrontal cortex (PFC) is one of the last parts of the brain to form in humans and is associated with the capacity to pay attention. Similar to a control panel, the PFC regulates things like problem-solving, planning, mental flexibility, directing attention and managing our emotions. One key function is the ability to imagine the future and recollect the past. This is crucial for our evolution and is the main reason for our success to adapt to and control the environment.

However, if we are unconscious, we lose the ability to differentiate between imagination and reality. Another part of the brain as the amygdala (fear center) can trick our thinking, and we lose the clarity and ability to get things done because of the activation of the flight or fight response.

Mindfulness and meditation help us to discern the reality of the present moment from our imaginative thoughts. The mind has the creativity to imagine things, but it won't confuse it anymore with the reality, making us able to focus on the present and experience those beautiful, imaginative thoughts in the reality of the present. Future can always be a result of our imagination. With mindfulness, we raise the chances to transform it into reality. As we understand that the future is just an image that we want to make a reality of, we focus our attention on the present. Mindfulness and meditation research shows changes in the area of the brain are associated with executive functioning, short-term memory, regulating emotions, planning, and mental flexibility. One of those mental flexibilities also includes the famous task of multitasking.

Multitasking

Most people think they can multitask which means focusing on two things simultaneously. The experiment shows that we are able to focus on two simple stimuli at the same time, for instance listening to basic sentences while pressing a button when a color pops up on the screen. When the tasks become more complex as talking to the phone while writing an email or trying to do a number of things at once, our brain divides the attention and starts doing what is called *attention switching*.

Research shows that our brain cannot handle more than one complex tasks at a time and there is a serious downside to operating this way. What happens when we multitask is that every time we switch our attention from one thing to another, there is a lag time of half a second where our visual attention is unable to notice anything new. If we think at every time, we stop focusing on something and check our email or Instagram or any other social website, we lose our concentration. Doing this enough time crucially disrupts our productivity. Other research shows that if we interrupt our work to check emails, it takes over a minute to get our full attention back to what we were originally doing. Making this problem even worse is that doing things in this way actually starts training our executive function to jump our attention from one thing to another rather than focusing for long periods of time on what really needs our attention. Most of us are doing it without even realizing it because it is hardwired into the brain. This crucially affects our productivity and so produces stress for not being able to get things done.

The solution to this is that before focusing on something, take a deep breath, set your phone on *airplane* mode, and try to leave all possible distractors (any stimuli as food, people, TV, etc.) away. You would still have your thoughts that will try to pull your attention away since you can't put them on airplane mode. Being mindful and gently bringing back your attention to the task by identifying thoughts without labeling or judging will help you not to get lost in the ocean of your thoughts.

Whether it's multitasking, problem-solving, or any other complicated brain task, we just cannot deny this power that machines work throughout our lives and are responsible for all almost all our actions. In the end, I'll leave you with my favorite quote by Amy Morin that emphasizes the value of the brain and how it can be used to promote productive thoughts and works in our lives.

"Wasting brain power ruminating about things you can't control drains mental energy quickly. The more you think about problems you can't solve, the less energy you'll have leftover for more productive endeavors."

-Amy Morin

Your Doodle Page

Your brain is like a machine that works round the clock and powers your body every single day. How do you utilize your brain power?

Chapter 8 - Give without Expectations of Receiving

"The true measure of a man is how he treats someone who can do him absolutely no good."

-Samuel Johnson

Some people say there's no such thing as a selfless act—that any time we do something to help another person, we get something in return, even if it's just a warm fuzzy feeling.

I've spent a lot of time playing with this idea in my head. It doesn't really bother me to know it feels good to help someone else. That, to me, is a completely acceptable type of selfishness. What gives me cause for concern are the underlying expectations we often have when we give *"selflessly."*

We've all been there. You cover for your coworker because you know you'll need her assistance next month. You give your sister $20, and then silently look for ways she can pay you back, even if not monetarily. You help your friend get leads for a job, and then feel angry when she isn't as proactive in offering you support. I've found that these expectations cause more stress than joy. They mar the act of giving, which makes me feel slightly guilty; they lead to disappointment if the person I helped doesn't return the kindness; and they tie my intentions to an internal scorecard, which places a wedge in my relationships. Recently I've been asking myself, *"What is my expectation?"* before I do something for another person.

The answer I find most acceptable, cheesy as it may sound, is to feel good and show love. Strangely, when I release the need to control what I get for giving, I get enough, somehow. When I was younger, I was brainwashed by society, that you always should give back or actually wait until someone gives you something to give back then.

Then I was in an ashram, and I contemplated nature, I realized the importance of giving, also through different books. What amazed me was how nature gives us everything without expecting from that epiphany I wanted to give all the time just for the purpose of giving, and that was enough for me, it helped me feel strong from the core. To get a grip on how physical the connections of your mind and personality are, let me tell you an interesting story.

I had a huge epiphany when I decided to climb a tree in the garden. So while I was walking, I climbed a tree and as I'm laying with my back on the tree and a start taking notes on my notebook I thought, wow this tree is giving me everything; the air I am breathing, the shade that I need, the food I eat and even then how do we treat nature? I took inspiration from that tree, and I said I want to be more like you, and start giving more. Notice that since then, I had a very greedy mind that was in control — always thinking about having more and keep more. After that day, I appreciate giving more than receiving.

The Science of Giving

The selfless part of our brain is considered a *deep brain structure* - part of the primitive or old brain. When we see a child or an older person in trouble, our first instinct is to spring into action and help them. Humans are social animals. So, it is nothing new that we are reinforced to help one another. In our modern complex society, there are numerous ways to give. The best part is that we understand that both the giver and the receiver benefit from this give-and-take kind of relationship. Neuroscience has established that giving is a powerful way of creating more personal happiness and improving well-being. While the brain is extraordinarily complicated, the neurochemical motivation for happiness is quite easy to recognize. Any activity that elevates the production of neurochemicals causes an improvement in mood. However, the advantages do not stop here. Serotonin is responsible for sleep, digestion, memory, learning, and appetite. Dopamine is responsible for motivation and arousal.

Oxytocin - the love hormone - is among the most primeval of our neurochemicals and has a powerful impact on the brain and the body. When it is released, blood pressure decreases and the basis for sexual arousal is cultivated. Affection increases, social fears are diminished, and trust and compassion are boosted. It is anti-inflammatory, decreases pain, and increases wound healing.

Hence, one wonders, if giving enables us to release all the chemicals at once, we owe it to ourselves to give as often as possible. Helping others can be done in many ways. Small repeated actions release the happy hormones thus encouraging you to help more and more. Opening a door, helping an old lady carry her grocery, helping a blind man cross the road, changing someone's tire, donating money for a cause, feeding a homeless man are all wonderful ways to give. Any time you go out of your way to help someone in need, you are automatically, unintentionally creating a bigger purpose for yourself.

Being generous to others triggers effects on our brain in many positive ways.

- **Compassion:** There is a network in the brain that helps us see things from the point of view of others. These mental procedures get some high pressure when you put yourself in the shoes of another person and try to give them what they need, without any personal benefit.

- **Neurons:** Being generous to others is often an appreciated social activity, which creates a wonderful cycle of giving. When you give, you make others happy because you are triggering their neurons. Both the giver and the receiver can directly affect the brain of the other in a positive way.

Helping others inspires the release of oxytocin, which has the power of enhancing your mood and combats the effects of cortisol - the stress hormone. Interestingly, the higher your level of oxytocin, the more is the need to help others. When oxytocin is released, so are serotonin, dopamine, and endorphins.

Do Good and Expect Nothing in Return

"Giving back is as good for you as it is for those you are helping because giving gives you purpose. When you have a purpose-driven life, you're a happier person."

-Goldie Hawn

Here we see, it is better to give than receive. The esteemed saying is incorporated into our heads from the day we gain consciousness. However, is there a deeper meaning to this quote? My answer to this is yes. Research provides compelling data to support the subjective evidence that giving is a powerful tool for personal growth and long-lasting happiness.

Through technology, we now understand that giving activates the same parts of the brain that are triggered by food and sex. As discussed above, selflessness is wired in our brains and is joyful. Helping others may just be the key to living a life that is not only happier but also healthier, wealthier, more optimistic, and productive. Helping others is an act of humanity and the proof of us being humans.

If your intention is to genuinely help others, then your entire focus should be on the word *others*. The idea of helping others is nothing like the give-and-take business. If we entertain the selfish motives or receiving something in return, even a *thank you*, the whole idea of helping loses its worth. Hence, it is said, *"Do a good deed and throw it into the well!"* Specifically meaning, do good and forget about it.

On one occasion, Jesus cured 10 lepers of their disease. Do you know how many of them expressed their gratitude and even said a simple thank you to Jesus? Just one. Jesus, then, turned to his disciples and inquired about the other nine. The disciples answered, *"Master, their selfish interest is satisfied and, therefore, they have now gone from here."* Jesus smiled and moved forward to help other people, telling his disciples, *"Do good unto others."* Help for the sake of helping.

Nature, as an example, gives us oxygen and fruit to live without expecting nothing. Nature also returns your goodness in unique ways. A poor farmer in Scotland, by the name of Fleming, one day heard a voice calling for help. He instantly ran following the voice for help and found a boy drowning in quicksand. Fleming struggled and pulled the boy out of the quicksand with some efforts. He warmly patted on his shoulder and told him to go back home. Then, he returned to his job. The next day, a wealthy gentleman visited the farmer and thanked him for saving the life of his son. He offered to reward the farmer. Fleming politely denied saying he had only done his duty. Looking at a little boy standing next to Fleming, the man asked if he was Fleming's son.

Fleming nodded and was told, *"This boy will make you proud one day."*

From that day onward, the wealthy gentleman took full responsibility for the education and upbringing of Fleming's son. This young boy grew up to be a famous scientist. He was Alexander Fleming. He helped humanity by his innovation of penicillin. A few months after the invention, the son of that gentleman was struck by a severe attack of pneumonia. Guess what?

His life was saved again with Fleming's invention - penicillin. This young boy was Winston Churchill. So you see, it is a fact, what goes around comes around. Nature does not preserve anything. Instead, it returns everything with interest. If the generous deed protracted by you to others is not retorted to you, the super conscience becomes triggered to make good happen to you. The very act of doing good is rewarding. It is not a business transaction that seeks profit or loss. So, do good without expecting anything in return. Nature will provide you with the benefit in some way or the other. When most people consider giving, they may have too constricted a focus.

All acts of giving work wonders, not only the cash donation given once or twice a year. Ask yourself, how can you help others? Is there a cause you can support? Does your friend need help? Is there a stranger who could benefit from your act of kindness? Do you have the ability to make someone's day?

You should fill each day with small acts of giving, as this is an actual way to bring happiness to yourself and others. Even just smiling at someone is an act of giving and brightens both of your days.

Your Doodle Page

Remind yourself of the time when you gave something to someone without expecting anything in return and how did that make you feel...

Chapter 9 – Nature

"Look deep into nature, and then you will understand everything better."

-Albert Einstein

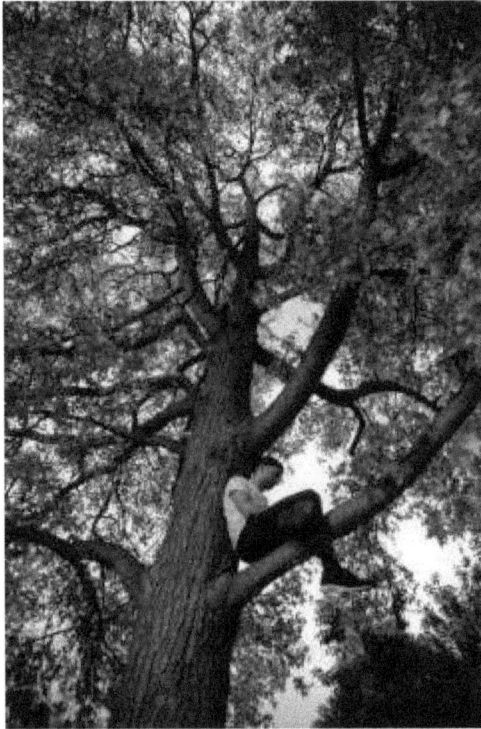

The earth, as you may know, is an unbelievably complicated and fragile system of interconnected structures that have evolved slowly over the last 4.5 billion years or so. From the dawn of the Big Bang, this planet appeared as a mass of energy and elements. From that, recently emerged forms of energy and components giving rise to organized, dynamic structures of solids, liquid, and gases. From the minutest organisms to the largest animals that came into being, every existence on earth is connected to some other existence. The birds are connected to the sky for the freedom to fly. We, humans, are connected to all other organisms for food and resources.

So how come mankind has come to dominate the earth in such a short period? Also, what gives us the power to do so? In precisely 3.5 billion years of life on earth, everything has led to a natural course of change. Our quick success as a species has started to affect this natural arrangement. With the current population at 7 billion and expanding, humans have played a huge role in the disorder of the earth's natural mechanism.

As we continue to breed and have a greater influence on the earth's mechanism, it is probable that we also tend to our role and relationship with nature to know why it is so important to be *one with nature*. Human's ability to influence the earth and realize the outcomes of doing so puts us in a strange position. As species, we have assumed the responsibility to provide and flourish. Our objective is to gain stability for our individual self and future generations. If you think about it long and hard, you also have a duty to take care of nature, as the humans depend on the resources and services nature provides.

The question now changes to *what part do we play in nature? How nature helps with shaping our behavior and habit? How can one find healing in nature?* To answer these questions, you must depend on your knowledge of earth, evolution, the power of nature, and how it affects humans in general.

History

Your relationship with nature has traditionally been one of disproportion and misuse. Almost every step in human history has regrettably been complemented with a rise in nature degradation. Initially, humans were in sync with nature. Ancient hunter tribes roamed the land, following the flow of life and the seasons. These tribes had a reasonable influence on nature and vice versa. With progress in technology and different fields, humans started to seek more successful ways of supporting themselves. These progressions enacted more permanent solutions, which was followed by an increase in population rate and a distance from nature. This dramatic shift to urban life involuntarily led to isolation from nature. While most people were still connected to nature on a competent level, the need for more and more resources started to transform the relationship with nature. While your isolation from nature began long ago with expansion in technology and social order, men of the past found peace and healing in its true form. They spent most of their time sitting in the wilderness and in the realms of nature reflecting on life's meaning and finding comfort in the divine through its creation.

Today, 8 out of 11 people accept that they are losing connection with nature. The pressure of everyday life means you are even more disconnected from nature even though nature, in many unique forms, is always there for you. It is true that, just like love, you are surrounded by nature at all times – and it's absolutely free.

If you think watching wildlife programs online or on the computer helps you connect to nature, you are wrong. It is no substitute for experiencing the calm and joy in nature directly. However, you do not necessarily have to go to the Amazon or the rainforest for experiencing nature. As amazing as those places are, nature is at your doorstep all year round. Simply add your curiosity, an amount of attention, and a scoop of patience, and watch your life transform in front of your eyes.

Importance of Nature

"Come forth into the light of things, Let nature be your teacher."

-William Wordsworth

Even William Wordsworth claims that nature is the best teacher. If you're looking for questions, trying to find the meaning of life, and can't handle the pressure of the material world, sit in nature and simply breathe. Nature is your best teacher. It teaches you lessons you didn't ask for but needed all the time. It heals your soul like it was never done. It opens your mind to numerous possibilities and clears the clutter to help you see the goodness and the positivity in front of you.

Nature, in all its forms and glory, brings you out of despair and leads you to a joyful place of calmness and serenity. Nature ignites the passion inside you. It moves your soul and gives wings to your spirit. Nature, with its beautiful landscapes, fills your heart and puts life in your ideas. Every day, experiences of nature enhance your life, increase your lifespan, and add value to your life. It feels like you are blessed with your free natural health treatment. The importance that nature had in my personal experience helped me become more creative and understand the science behind the benefit of staying around nature. There is no doubt that the earth has been a generous planet. Everything you need to live and nurture is given by nature surrounding us - food, water, medicine, shelter, and even natural system of seasons. Researchers call this phenomenon *ecosystem services*.

The realization of such services trace back to some thousands of years and maybe even beyond if one agrees to the ancient cave paintings as proof. Now, we have detached ourselves from nature so much that it is easy, and often suitable, to overlook that nature remains as generous as ever, even it disappears gradually.

The advancement of technology and economics may have isolated us ignorantly from nature, but it has been unable to change our dependence on the natural environment. Most of what we are surrounded by and use regularly are the products of multiple connections within nature, and many of these connections are endangered. Apart from physical benefits, nature also provides less-tangible, yet essential, gifts regarding beauty, aesthetics, art, healing, and spirituality.

I decided to live my life without social media that helped me a lot having the time to actually go in nature and keep myself indulged in it. I decided to come closer to nature by moving in a place close to the gardens and the beach. So every time I go for a walk, I am surrounded by both, and then I realized the importance of the solid ground beneath our feet and walking barefoot on the grass or the sand, which really changed my life. I felt more energies aligning with my soul and body, making for at ease with myself. Additionally, I also derived a huge boost of creativity every time I was in nature... I wrote or drew or made music, and you could feel the difference from when you do it in a room.

I love nature as I love myself. This is the reason why I am starting a clothing label made with eco-sustainable clothing. The clothing line will use different approaches with material like hemp and organic cotton because I want to make people realize first that there are many options to the way we do things and second that the fashion industry is the second largest industry for pollution, all this synthetic material that not only harm the environment but also us. I also decided to include whole plant-based food in my diet. I was curious to try to be vegetarian or vegan. Then I was looking for a new room to live in because my lease was over and the house I was interested in was supposed to be shared with this vegan guy. So, I took the challenge and now it has been almost one year that I haven't eaten any meat or animal product. I loved cheese on my pasta and my burgers, but honestly, I didn't know about so many options that let me do this transition effortlessly. The difference between whole plant-based food and vegan is that whole plant-based food is eating what nature wholly give you so that the ideal would be having your own garden.

So we basically don't eat anything that is also processed to eliminate the waste of plastic that is killing our planet. April 22, Earth Day, appears as a good day to remind ourselves of the things that nature has blessed us with, free of any cost. Here is a glimpse of how important nature is in different aspects of our life.

Health

Recent studies have discovered what nature-enthusiasts have long hoped for. Passing the time in a yard or a park offers advantages for both mental and physical health. Morning exercises in a park, instead of a gym, has proven to deliver mental health benefits as a bigger part of your well-being. Walking for 30 minutes in a park has been evident to assist children with ADHD and enhance their focus as well as functioning. People who spend more time in nature have improved their overall health, even when research considered recent economic differences. The benefits of nature are abundant. From healing your sickness to improving your moods, nature is the antidote to all of your complications.

It Improves Your Mood

Starting your day by basking in the warm sunlight is a great way to bring a smile to your face. Sunlight is responsible for providing you with vitamin D, which is scientifically proven to improve your mood, relax the nervous system, and increase bone strength. Apart from this, vitamin D from the sun also endorses the absorption of calcium in the body. Receiving a good amount of it can also reduce the risk of high blood pressure, cancer, and other autoimmune diseases.

It Brings You to the Present Moment

Disconnecting from your regular life and stepping outdoors enables you to focus on the present. At the most basic level, connecting with nature inspires you to live in the present moment, calm your mind, and breathe in the natural sounds, smells, and sights that surround you. Basic knowledge of meditation, getting your focus to the present – instead of regretting over past or worrying about the future – can exceptionally reduce stress and anxiety.

It Boosts Your Energy

While you may consider that a strong espresso is a secret to overcoming an afternoon setback, studies suggest that a 20-minute walk in a park is a better and cheaper option. Several studies printed in the *Journal of Environmental Psychology* stated that individuals who spent as little as 20 minutes a day in nature experienced increased energy level and a boost in their overall mood than those who did not.

It Heals You

Dwelling on nature or simply viewing sights of nature reduces anger, fear, anxiety, stress, and triggers pleasant feelings. Contact with nature not only makes you feel better emotionally but also adds to your physical well-being, decreasing hypertension, heart rate, muscle tension, and the release of stress hormones. According to researchers, it may also reduce mortality. They suggest that even a single plant or a picture of a beautiful scene has a significant effect on stress and anxiety.

It Improves Memory

A good memory can be a crucial asset when it comes to realizing your creative ability. A strong memory can help you generate new ideas and come up with unique and creative solutions that you may not have come up with otherwise. The University of Michigan conducted research on their students and discovered that those who spent more time in nature showed signs of a strong memory and increased productivity.

It Enhances Brain Function

For your brain to function properly at its maximum level, you need to be able to decrease lethargy and increase your energy level. This allows your brain to repair itself so you can start thinking of new ideas and involving in your highest analytical abilities. As per the *Journal of Environmental Psychology*, only 20 minutes a day outside is all you may need to push your brain to revive, restore, and start functioning again.

It Improves Mental Health

If you are suffering from poor mental health, you will never be able to achieve your creative potential. Spending some time in nature can help improve your mood and boost your overall mental health in general.

In a study published by the mental health organization known as MIND, contributors were either consigned to go for a walk in nature or in a museum. The study discovered that 71 percent of volunteers had fewer symptoms of depression after their walk in nature. The people who walked through the museum, 22 percent of them were even more depressed after their walk.

Art

Think of a yard without flowers, poetry without prose, painting without colors, or a film without a story. What if Shakespeare had no rose to relate Juliet to, or if John Keats' poetries lacked romance? What if Van Gogh ran out of stars to paint or Durer an animal to slaughter? Imagine the *Jungle Book* without *Bagheera* or *The Lion King* without *Zazu*. There is indeed no doubt that nature has gifted its universal blessings to us with some of its highest subjects. If you lose in nature, you will lose in all of its art.

Ancient Roman philosopher, Cicero, once stated: *"Art embraces those things of which we have knowledge."* In ancient Greek, this idea was quite common, considering art was the unique act of creating things according to the rules - to be specific, the existing norms of nature. The Greeks considered nature pure perfection, and mankind could not follow anything outside nature's asserted laws.

Addressing the idea of original thought in ancient days was viewed as outrageous, sometimes even absurd. The Greeks believed that the artist was not a creator, but a wanderer, a discoverer of art from nature's laws. All of this changed at the dawn of the renaissance when the liberty to discover new thought and ideas – to create unique work outside nature's proclaimed laws – started to become standard. Even after then, creativity was thought to exist only as a foreign act, granted to humans by divine power.

The simple act of creation was developed from basically nothing. Hence, the term *divine inspiration* came into being. There was no way to consider how new ideas could naturally occur in the brain. As time advanced so did human's knowledge of the brain, and simultaneously understanding of the ways thoughts are created. Presently, we live in an age where creativity is appreciated and understood not to be a divine inspiration but an act done by artists, poets, and painters only. Creativity is, in reality, a naturally existing process in the human brain - the fixing together of supposedly unconnected notion to give room to new ones. There are still innumerable creatives who affirm that creativity is something almost magical. Why do you think is that? Magic is instilled into creativity because at its very basic, we still don't understand how it really functions. Researchers and neurologists of the present don't completely understand how our thoughts are formed and further expand in the brain.

They simply know that thoughts do. Considering this idea, creativity is a lot like the air we breathe. Even if you recognize it and know that there is nothing magical, that doesn't make it any easier to see it. There is, however, still a lot of secrecy and misunderstanding to creativity, yet it surprises many of us every day. It transforms the way we use our phones, it protects lives, and it inspires, motivates, and prevents us from sleeping at night. Maybe, irrespective of scientific understanding, there is some other foreign and ghostly power incorporating inspiration in us. That marvel is what truly makes the process magical.

If you ever had a day job, you probably had that one moment where you looked outside of the window and thought you could do a lot more, perform better, and accomplish new and better things if you only had a few minutes outdoors. Regardless, you long for a breath of fresh air or a walk into the woods. There is nothing like the temptation of nature when you are trapped struggling to make it through the day.

While most people long to spend some time in nature just to relax or take a break from their regular 9-5 job, there are numerous studies that found that connecting with nature is a great way to boost your creativity. Stanford University conducted research and concluded that when people spend time in nature, they experience an extraordinary shift in their perception of time. To be precise, when you spend time in nature, you feel as if time is paused or expanding.

Despite feeling stressed out by time or not having enough time, people feel an abundance of time when they are connected with nature. Being a part of nature not only helps you reduce anxiety but it can also assist you in finding that inspiration you are seeking in your everyday tasks. Nothing is as stressing out as having a tight deadline and being hindered with a creative block. The good news is that spending quality time in nature can help open the door for new ideas to come through.

Spirituality

While some of what nature provides you is measurable, most of what it gives you is simply infinite. Economic dimensions are important, but in regard to most of the things that happen in the world, economics is simply unqualified of capturing its true value. Science is also important in regard to the importance of human nature, but then again it cannot measure the true meaning of nature. Probably, the most complicated gift of nature is to measure its deep-rooted relation to human spirituality. In many religions, nature is rightly admired.

In Christianity, worldly heaven occurred in the form of a yard, while God ordered Noah, the initial preservationist to preserve every species. Buddhists are of the view that every organism – from the smallest ant to the biggest whale – holds and is worthy of reverence. For Hindus, every aspect of the natural world is instilled with spirituality. Muslims, on the other hand, believe that nature was created by their one God, Allah, and offered to humans as a gift to be apprehended in faith.

Ethnic cultures all over the world celebrate nature as their *mother* – treated with the utmost respect and the highest form of healing and spirituality. However, you don't have to be religious to acknowledge the importance of nature to the human soul. You only need to spend time alone in a forest, sit on a rustic bench, forget about deadlines, phone calls, and meetings, trace your fingers on the veins of leaves, watch the sun shower the flowers, trees, and birds with its rays, and surrender into the serenity that nature has to offer to you.

You may not be aware, but nature has a strong connection with your spiritual side, helping you gain a stronger sense of yourself. You may be a huge part of a universe larger than you could even imagine, but that doesn't mean you can't seek relief in the environment surrounding you. Find your connection by doing things as simple as walking without purpose over a moist forest floor or dipping your toes in the river.

Nature executes big miracles for us each day, from blessing us with breathtaking views and helping to prevent natural disasters to controlling the weather and supplying us with fresher, cleaner air to breathe, and not to forget the abundant food. When taking a shower or performing your daily chores, it's easy to overlook that without good soil.

Trees are made to cool us in hot weathers and overtake air pollution. You have fresh produce on your table that was cultivated in nature. Bees pollinate your crops to provide you with honey – one of the many delicacies of nature, and so much more that is impossible for you to fathom. Without nature and a healthy environment, you will be as lost as a tourist in a foreign country without a map.

So, the next time you find yourself struggling to bring some ideas to your work, try spending some time in nature. It may be more beneficial than sitting in your four-walled, dark, and boring office hoping for ideas to flow to you. Take a deep breath, inhale the freshness and goodness of nature, and let it linger through your body gradually, infiltrating into your veins positivity and nothing but compassion and creativity.

Your Doodle Page

Has spending time in nature helped you think better and overcome your struggles? Think and write below:

Chapter 10 - Telepathy

"In spiritual communication, mental telepathy is the beginners' course."

-Sri Chinmoy

Telepathy is the direct transmission of thoughts from one person to another without using the common sensory modes of communications, therefore is a type of extrasensory perception (ESP). While the presence of telepathy is not yet verified, a few psychological types of research have indicated favorable results using this technique. I always knew about telepathy because I grew up with two sisters, and sometimes it happened that we had the same dream or that we thought about the same thing at the same time.

So I started practicing more and eventually with my closest friend. Sometimes I would receive a text in the night while my phone was off, then I would wake up with a dream of that person that texted me. Crazy thing, but I realize that most of the time, I don't need to talk to express how I feel about something with the people that are close to me. Just a look, and they would understand what I am thinking.

The process of conveying thoughts from one mind to another, i.e., mental telepathy, has customarily occupied the domains of both science and mysticism, either of which is foreign to conventional science. However, research in 2014 completely changed that with a logically proven demonstration of telepathic communication. A neuroscientist from the University of Barcelona conducted an experiment in which signals received by an electroencephalograph (EEG) from senders in India were sent over the internet as email messages to receivers in France where the scalps had been fixed with Transcranial Magnetic Stimulators (TMS).

These devices have been long used to cure anxiety and depression, and trigger mental activity in the brain through intact connection utilizing strong magnetic fields. The TMS stimulators in this experiment were located over the occipital cortex at the lower back of the brain, producing a superficial flash of light, known as phosphene, through neural stimulations in the visual cortex. The participants in India were taught to release an EEG signal signifying either 1 or 0 making use of the biofeedback monitor. A 1 was released when participants thought of moving a hand, while a 0 was produced when they thought of moving their foot.

These 1s and 0s were then emailed all the way from India to France and directed to one of two TMS devices fixed on the student's scalps. 1s were directed to a TMS electrode that caused a phosphene to be perceived, while 0s were directed to a different TMS device whose activity generated no phosphenes.

It concluded that the experiment was successful. Mistake rate of transmission ranged from between 1 and 11 percent, quite below what would be projected by random noise. But why should you care about that? Because one way of perceiving this experiment is that it is as celebrated as Alexander Graham Bell saying, *"Watson, come here, I want to look at you."* It was the first ever interaction over the telephone.

If telepathic communication is proven, it is possible that you will learn to communicate simple ideas and implications that texts, speeches, and facial expressions cannot, transforming the way humans connect to each other by strengthening and enriching the depth of communication. Sometimes, our words fail us, though our thoughts may not. Telepathy is useful in love and in every relationship. So many times, I found myself without need to talk that the person I am with already knowing what I am feeling of what

I wanted to express without saying a word. That helps with the creation of projects when I collaborate with different artists as well.

Simple Definition of Telepathy

Telepathy explains receiving thoughts or feelings from a person at a certain distance, without the use of any of the five common senses of sight, touch, taste, hearing, and smell. It is more probable to occur between two people who already share a close relationship.

Twins often report that they can sense each other's feelings, irrespective of the distance between them. Somehow they seem to have a programmed birth link. It is, however, possible to have this mode of communication with almost anyone. Surprisingly, some people can also connect telepathically to animals.

A telepathic relationship is derived from the concept that all organisms originate from the same foundation - some call this a spiritual basis, others a natural source, and others a universal foundation.

Who is Telepathic?

Every one of us is born with a telepathic gift. It is learning and practicing how to use this gift that stops many of us from being able to communicate effectively. Lack of knowledge, uncertainty, and general societal perceptions are often huge components in the people blocking this unique intuitive ability.

Some cultures of the world openly accept communication in this manner. For example, the Japanese specifically use this word to describe the relationship between lovers that is developed from this telepathic indulgence.

Learn to Communicate with Telepathy

A composed state increases telepathic powers. Meditation greatly helps to calm the mind and body. It also makes you more accessible to receiving and sending telepathic communications. It helps with decluttering your mind from irrelevant and unnecessary thoughts too. Open-mindedness increases the chances of telepathic communications whereas a closed mind is less probable to be able to transfer or receive successfully.

Avoid listening to those who doubt your abilities. Once you start believing in yourself, do not let others transform your views with their skepticism and negativity. When trying to deliver a message telepathically, imagine the receiver in great detail. Visualize them standing in front of you and you transmitting your message. Imagine that you are talking to them over a phone call. The following are a few important components that enable successful communication with telepathy.

Patience

When indulging in telepathy, do not forget that just like any other skill, practice makes it perfect. Do not anticipate instant results in one or two days. Your intuitive power will improve with practice.

Health

Improved overall health and well-being is useful for successful communication. Everything is feebler when you are mentally and physically sick, including your ability to transmit thoughts and feelings.

Ensuring It Works Well

As you deliver your thoughts, you naturally get a feeling that your message has been delivered. When this happens, stop directing your thoughts. If you are on the receiving end of a telepathic message from another person, you may sense that maybe you are imagining things. This is quite normal, but do not ignore the signals. Listen to them and keep them safe in your memory.

Advantages of Telepathy

When you are able to connect with other people, you can easily relate to them at a higher level, and a greater understanding is developed. This can have a huge impact on all your relationships. In regard to animals, you can understand the needs and wants of your favorite pet, who are unable to communicate with you verbally.

Animals can sometimes sense a threat before they become too obvious. Knowing the feelings of animals can protect you against potentially dangerous circumstances. The technique of telepathy provides successful and efficient means of communication. It is eco-friendly and free of cost. In this, the location of the recipient and sender does not matter. Imagine you want to get in touch with someone in a far land, but fail due to the bad internet connection. Don't worry, you no longer have to rely on poor connections or weak mobile signals to do so.

- You can communicate with plants, animals, and even other beings such as dead people, spirits, the divine self, and even the angelic empire.
- Telepathy is more accurate for communications than speaking verbally. Have you ever felt someone saying one thing yet sending you a different message? This is not possible in telepathic communications.

Blocking Telepathic Communications

In case you don't know, it is possible to block others from being able to send or receive telepathic communications to and from you. You can lock your brain doors to one specific person. This, however, needs a lot of work on your part, as it is possible that you become so in sync with another person that sharing your thoughts become an automatic process. Despite using telepathy for mind-to-mind communication, you can communicate with almost any living organism. We all have, in some way, communicated telepathically with friends, family, co-workers, and even animals and plants, and may not be even aware of doing so. Learning how to build your telepathic ability requires a lot of practice, but is also quite easy and can be opted by anyone with an open mind.

Who Are You: Sender or Receiver?

You may not know but some of you are stronger receivers of information, and some of you are able to send messages efficiently than others. There are benefits of telepathy both for a sender as well as a receiver.

If You Are a Natural Sender, Then...

- If you are thinking about how great it would be if someone brings you a hot cup of coffee; to your surprise, a friend may stop by to drop some coffee and bagel.
- People feel influenced by your mood swings.
- Your pet could listen to and follow you without you speaking any word.

If You Are a Natural Receiver, Then...

- You can pick up grocery or some items that someone at home may need but is unable to contact you or ask you to pick for them.

- You can get in touch with an old friend or a family member when they are thinking about you.

- Solutions to your problems naturally flow to you without any hard work.

- People often tell you that you take the words out of their mouth before they could even speak.

How You Can Develop Your Telepathic Ability

Practice with Someone You're Close

Practicing telepathy with someone you are close is a great way to develop your telepathic ability. Decide who will be the sender and the receiver. Once you decide and are well-versed in the process, swap roles to practice different positions.

Start Gradually

Start by sending simple and easy messages such as one number a day or one color or shape at an agreed time that is convenient for both parties. Gradually, pick up the pace and move to the next level. A week later, send bigger words or sentences.

Believe in Your Potential

Believe that you can work on your telepathic gifts and polish them through practice. When you doubt yourself, you are preventing the entire process. Making use of positive affirmations such as *'Telepathy is easy for me to master and I shall do this with confidence and ease'* will instantly boost your spirit.

Calm Your Mind

When your mind is calm and your body is relaxed, the messages, images, and signals will flow through you without any effort. Free yourself of all the worldly chaos, and make sure your focus is on practicing the skill only. External factors will only hinder the process.

Use All Your Strength and Let It Go

When you are sending a thought, send it with all your energy. However, once you have let it go, don't spend time thinking about it anymore. By not pondering over the thought again, you are starting afresh and making it easy for the receiver to receive the message clearly and without any confusion.

Imagination

Hearing guiding meditations will assist you in building your imagination skills. If you want to be an efficient sender, you must be able to see the object or color clearly before sending it through. Meditation will only help you strengthen and speed up the process.

Don't Second-guess Your Abilities

When you are in the role of a receiver, go with the first thought and don't waste time in overthinking it. Distance your ego and mind from the process and believe whatever you are receiving is the correct information.

Work on Your Brain to Develop Telepathy

For mastering this kind of ability, a high amount of concentration and focus is needed. Training your mind is the main component that can help you communicate effectively. Normally, you use only 10 percent of your brain's capacity. However, for communicating with someone through telepathy, you need to use more than just 10 percent.

However, how can you train yourself to use your brain's fullest capacity when all your life, 90 percent of your brain has remained futile? The answer is simple. Finding balance in your life will help a lot when it comes to finding the right direction to invest our energy in. Once the art of finding and maintaining balance is mastered, you will be able to expand the power of your mind to greater heights.

It is then when we see the difference in inherent telepathic abilities, but in addition you will also observe a stark advancement in overall life.

Attaining the Highest Level of Communication

"Communication means sharing together, thinking together, not agreeing or disagreeing together but thinking,

*observing, learning and understanding together. Both you
and the speaker have to take the journey together. "*

-J. Krishnamurti

What more does a person want than to be able to
communicate effectively and be understood with clarity by
other people? This can be achieved easily with the help of
Empathic Telepathy. This is the highest level of
communication that can be learned and achieved. The
communication that we are used to generally requires and is
limited by the time-space continuum. Using Empathic
Telepathy, we can communicate all the rich information
which is beyond any language, regardless of time and space.

Unsurprisingly, this certain ability has been coded in our
genes since the first human was created. What does this
mean? You and all other individuals are perfectly capable of
not only unlocking this special mode of communication but
also enhancing its effectiveness and power. The fact that you
can sometimes sense what a person who's close to you is
thinking and feeling means that you have already unlocked
this ability naturally.

So, how can you enhance this kind of communication? Who can act as your teacher and guide?

"The nature of ignorance is to lack deep communication with the universe. It is to separate, to isolate, to create discrimination and differences so that finally we cannot communicate as a harmonious whole. These differences we create appear as fighting, anger, hatred and war."

Nature is indeed the best teacher. So, sit by a tree and relax, opening your mind to vulnerable connection and communication. However, you still need to do take care of a few things to master this form of telepathy.

Tips to Master Telepathy

Here are a few useful tips for you to successfully master telepathy.

- For starters, keep your experiment precise.
- 15 minutes or less is a perfect time for the exercise. Any time phase more than this will hinder your progress and your ability to communicate effectively.
- Have a high level of energy.
- Maintain patience.

Similar to everything else in life, you need to be patient to see the best results. You might not see any progress in the beginning, but with practice and strong will, you will surely see good results sooner or later. Finally, have faith that you can achieve it and stay away from all sorts of negativity.

Negative people only bring your energy down, put doubt in your mind, and carve your spirits. It's your job to show them how determined you are through your accomplishments and achievements. Try not to get discouraged. Staying positive and practicing positivity is the key to effective telepathy.

Your Doodle Page

Connecting with other people is nothing short of a miracle. List down the attempts you have made in life to connect with people and how it helped you in life:

Chapter 11 - Step Out of Your Comfort Zone

"You never change your life until you step out of your comfort zone; change begins at the end of your comfort zone."

-Roy T. Bennett

You've probably seen inspiring quotes that urge you to get outdoors and do something with your life – something different – something unique – but stepping out of your comfort zone takes so much hard work. Basically, there is a science behind this notion that explains why it's so difficult to break out of your comfort zone and why it's the best thing you can ever do.

With a little knowledge and few amendments, you can easily break free from your mundane routine and do amazing things. It just requires taking the first step. I remember when I first came to Australia as an immigrant; I did not know how to speak English. I had trouble making friends. I did not know my way around - anything. It was difficult, even I thought stepping out into the unknown was even scarier.

Basically, I did not know how to step out of my comfort zone because I thought I had everything I needed. I enjoyed my own company back then. Also, the first time I performed a poem on a stage, I was terrified by the crowd. So nervous that I couldn't even hold my poem without shaking. Same as the first time I have been busking and actually sing and rap in front of so many strangers. The feeling you experience could really not be described by words. Stepping out of your comfort zone is strange yet amazing, and I invite everybody to do it at least once.

To most people, this sort of behavior is very egocentric and selfish. However, all of that changed when I eventually moved to Malibu. I finally decided to step out of my comfort zone. I believe that was the turning point in my life. I started to befriend more people. I learned new things. I began teaching yoga and started my journey to become a public speaker, all at the age of 22. I loved how simply stepping out of my comfort zone increased my productivity, how I was able to help other people with their mental health problems and set a good example for people of my age.

I became so interested in reading books that they helped me change my environment and everything around me that was negative and stopping me from moving forward. I believed in myself and started meditating. I learned that the ego that was driving me most of my life was stopping me from being productive.

My dream, initially, was to make money. I egoistically made the act of making money my one and only goal. However, after stepping out of my comfort zone, I became more spiritual and my goals changed. The more connected and aligned I felt with myself, the more I wanted to help other people with stepping out of their comfort zone. So, it is very important to extend the boundaries of your comfort zone.

However, what exactly is the comfort zone? Why is it that you get so comfortable with your daily routine and fear even the slightest change? What benefits do you attain from ultimately breaking out of your comfort zone, and how exactly do you go about it? Finding answers to these questions is a lengthy task, but that does not mean it's impossible.

The Science behind Comfort Zone and Why It's Hard to Leave It

To be precise, your comfort zone is a social space where your activities and behaviors match a routine and similar patterns that reduce stress, anxiety, and any risk. It offers a state of mental security where you benefit in obvious manners - constant happiness, low anxiety, and less stress.

The concept of comfort zone stretches back to a traditional experiment in psychology. In 1908, psychologists John D. Dodson and Robert M. Yerkes described that a state of comfort gave rise to a stable level of performance. To improve your performance, you need to find a state of relative anxiety – a place where your stress level is comparatively higher than usual. This particular space is referred to as *optimal anxiety*, and it's simply outside your comfort zone.

With too much pressure, you feel too stressed to be productive, and your performance automatically declines to a great level. The concept of optimal anxiety is not new. Any person who has ever pushed themselves to get to the next level or accomplish something new knows that when you really challenge yourself, you receive significantly amazing outcomes. However, pushing yourself too hard can also bring a negative outcome and strengthen the idea that challenging yourself is indeed a bad idea. As humans, it is your natural tendency to remain in your familiar and comfortable state. So now, you can understand why it is so hard to push yourself out of your original comfort zone. Your comfort zone is neither a bad nor a good thing. It's a natural state that most people drift toward.

Abandoning it refers to increased risk and anxiety, which can show both positive and negative outcomes but don't demean your comfort zone in regard to holding you back. You all need that personal space where you are less anxious and less stressed so you can easily process the benefits you get when you leave it.

This Is What You Get When You Step Out of Your Comfort Zone and Try New Things

Optimal anxiety is the space where your mental effectiveness and performance reach its peak. Yes, *increased performance* and *improved productivity* are similar to doing more work. So what do you really get when you step out of your comfort zone and try new things?

You'll Be More Effective

In case you don't know, comfort kills productivity. Without the idea of anxiety that comes from deadlines and expectations, you tend to do the least required to get through. You lose the passion and ambition to do more and learn new things. Pushing your boundary can help you hit your goal sooner and seek smarter ways to work.

You'll Be More Comfortable in Dealing with New and Drastic Changes

An article, published in The New York Times by a professor from the University of Houston, explains that one of the worst things you can do is pretend to be scared and believe that uncertainty doesn't exist. By accepting risks in a controlled manner and challenging yourself to adventures you normally wouldn't opt for, you can actually experience some of that uncertainty in a relaxed yet certain way. Learning to step out of your comfort zone when you are preparing for life's biggest challenges can be an amazing trip if you think about it.

You'll Find It Easier in the Future

Once you practice stepping out of your comfort zone, it will get better with time. You eventually become used to that primal state of optimal anxiety. You become more familiar with it, and you're willing to push more before your performance drops.

You Can Brainstorm Easily and Foster Creativity

This is another advantage but is also common sense that searching for new experiences, practicing new abilities, and accepting new opportunities inspire you and motivate you than anything else does.

Trying New Tasks Can Help You Reflect

Trying new tasks can help with reflecting on previous decisions and inspire you to learn more from mistakes and bad experiences. Even in the short term, it can help you brainstorm new ideas, view old problems in a new and brighter light, and face hardships with new energy. The advantages you get from stepping out of your comfort zone linger for longer periods of time. First, there's an overall boost you get through the skills you learn, the new experiences you live, the new food you devour, the new countries you visit, and the new job you apply for. There are other mental benefits you receive from expanding your horizons.

It's Okay to Visit Your Comfort Zone from Time to Time

You can't stay outside your comfort zone for a long time. You have to pay it a visit from time to time to process the things you learned. You don't want your new-found place to become common and boring. This spectacle, known as *hedonistic adaptation,* is the natural propensity to be enthralled by new things only to have the extraordinary become ordinary after a short time.

It is how you can have access to the greatest inventory of human knowledge ever constructed – the internet – at your fingertips and get so dull that all we consider is how fast we can get newer and more advanced access. In a way, it drives us forward, but in another way, it prevents us from appreciating the simple and everyday tasks. However, you can survive this by trying unique but smaller things.

Start by ordering a new dish at the restaurant where you order the same dish on every visit. Similarly, traveling to a new country can be both an eye-opening experience and a great way to step out of your comfort zone. Broaden the challenges you face so you're not just pushing your boundaries in the same direction over and over again. If you're learning French and after some time, find yourself completely bored, switch gears and move to something new. You never know what might ignite the spark in you. If you've decided to start exercising, instead of just doing push-ups and regular exercise, push yourself to a new level every time you cross the previous one. In a way, you're still challenging yourself but on different levels of comfort.

Make Stepping Out of Your Comfort Zone a Permanent Habit

The reason to step out of your comfort zone is to embark on new experiences and attain the state of optimal anxiety in a convenient way, not to stress yourself out. Spend some time reflecting on your experiences, so it's easy for you to read the benefits and implement to your daily activities. You can always do something new and even more interesting. Try to make it a habit. Practice something new every week or every month. Put your boundaries to the real test by trying something new regularly. Remember, not to confine yourself to huge, expensive, and time-consuming experiences. Perhaps, meditation pushes you out of your comfort zone as much as skydiving does. So, try the latter if you've already done the former. Your purpose is not to become a professional. You just need to find out what you're capable of doing well. There is another reason why it's crucial to return to a safe and comfortable state at times. Don't forget to bring back as much as you can take from those high spirited, creative, inspired, and sometimes uncomfortable moments.

Why You Need to Step Out of Your Comfort Zone

You're inspired, you're ambitious, you've big plans in the pipeline, and you're taking big steps to reach your goals. Life is going great, maybe even better than you hoped for. The comfort zone you're lounging in is convenient. You've been successful in accomplishing great things within its boundaries. You comfort zone is similar to your home. It's comfortable, relaxing, and can be a space infusing productivity and success. What happens when you trip on a rock that makes you scream - uncomfortable? The thought of leaving your home - your happy place - can be overwhelming. But the world is a dangerous place. What if you get lost? What if you get hurt? What if you run into the wrong people? It's a fact that outside your safe little space, any of these calamities can happen. Deciding to stay inside is a good way to avoid them. But if you ever meander outside, you'll have a series of wonderful experiences the universe has to offer.

Most of you have a picture of the comfort zone as a fragment of encouragement psychology and a tagline of cheesy advertisements 'strive for success.' However, in reality, the comfort zone is a valuable psychological idea that can help embrace risk and make changes to your life that can guide you to personal growth.

Your comfort zone, as explained by the experts, is a *developmental space* where your activities and behaviors match a routine and structure that reduce stress and risk. In your comfort zone, you feel secure, familiar, and confident. When you walk outside that comfortable space, you're taking a risk and opening yourself to new opportunities of stress and anxiety, since you're not sure of what awaits you outside that zone.

Since the beginning of time, you are made to accept that stress is a negative emotion but a little stress can actually play the part of a catalyst for progress and powerful motivation. Generally stating, even within your comfort zone is a little stress that you're unaware of. According to research, the idea of a *comfort zone* was introduced in regard to the temperature zone (67-78 degrees) - the optimum temperature where you feel neither hot nor cold.

While your comfort zone can be convenient, productive, and familiar, stepping out of it into new opportunities and challenges can create conditions that reward you with maximum productivity. Ask yourself, have you ever been able to do something productive in autopilot mode? In a progressively competitive, dangerous, and fast-moving world, people who voluntarily take risks, constantly try new things, and step out of their comfort zone into the discomforts of the real world reap the biggest benefits.

I'm not suggesting there's anything wrong with living in your comfort zone, until the point you get too comfortable and start holding yourself back instead of pushing yourself to learn, grow, and produce more. Being somewhat uncomfortable, whether by will, can encourage you to achieve goals you never thought you could. However, it's crucial that you don't challenge yourself and be productive at all times. It's a good idea to step out of your comfort zone, but it's also good to step back in and test your choices.

Challenge Yourself to Perform Your Best

Getting out of your comfort zone is the most crucial factor in your overall growth. Think about it: how can you expect to transform if you stick to the same old routine? Achieving great things requires the risk of trying something. A little anxiety can help you give your best. In short, when you challenge yourself, you incline to rise.

Taking Risks Helps You Reach the Peak

As a child, you're a natural risk-taker. As you grow into adulthood and develop a fear of failure, you start stopping yourself from trying new things. This comes at a huge cost to your remarkable potential for growth and evolution. The fear that holds you back is the biggest obstacle to your growth. It guarantees the progressive decline of your personality and stops your need to explore and experiment. There is absolutely no learning without effort and hard work. If you want to learn and explore, you must continue to take risks, all your life. It doesn't get simpler than that.

Stepping Out of Your Comfort Zone Can Make You Creative

Creativity is naturally very risky. When you show your creativity to the world, you are automatically opening yourself to vulnerable situations and even possible criticism. Simultaneously, risking setbacks heightens the possibility of great creative accomplishments. Creative people fail and the best ones fail quite often.

Stepping out of your comfort zone once in a while makes it easier and more probable that you'll do it again. Research in 2012 discovered that students who studied abroad were reported to be more creative than those who did not. Students who spent a semester in a foreign country away from home scored higher on two different creativity tests than students who studied in their home towns.

To become a person who takes frequently measured risks, challenge yourself and try new things. Show open-mindedness to new experiences – one of psychology's Big Five personality characteristics. Being open to new experiences is similar to qualities like curiosity, intellect, visualization, emotional interest, and the desire to explore your inner and external interests. It is proved to be the best interpreter for creative accomplishments.

Age Better by Embracing New Possibilities

With time, your comfort zone diminishes, but if you continue to expand it, you'll allow yourself to benefit from greater satisfaction and improved health as you grow older. Research at the University of Texas discovered that cultivating new and challenging life skills, while upholding a strong social network can help you stay healthy mentally and physically as you age.

The research concluded that committing alone is not enough. The research constantly encouraged a group of people to learn new skills, challenge themselves, and master new tasks. Only the people who faced many new risks and mental challenges were able to improve their mental state.

Don't Be Too Hard on Yourself

It has been found that stimulation improves performance but to a certain limit. When performance is enhanced when worked up to the level of optimal anxiety, after that, it only creates stress and more anxiety. When there is more demand than you can handle, the pressure overwhelms you. With little time and support, you enter the proximity of stress and restlessness. Just after the optimal anxiety zone is the declining point where your brain releases too many stress hormones that start to restrict your ability to work well, to learn, to master a new skill, to be creative, to listen, and to plan. Obviously, too much stress and anxiety can be deadly. Stress decreases your productivity and hinders creativity. Not to forget it contributes to a series of physical and mental diseases.

It might seem really scary in the beginning to get out of your comfort zone suddenly, but as you know, you don't have to jump right out of it, you can always start with small baby steps. As you gradually push past your comfort zone, you will start feeling more and more at ease about the new situations which previously appeared so dangerous to you. So, don't hesitate. Take the first step, and you'll definitely make it to your destination.

"I have learned in my life that it's important to be able to step outside your comfort zone and be challenged with something you aren't familiar or accustomed to. That challenge will allow you to see what you can do."

-J.R. Martinez

Your Doodle Page

Accepting new challenges in life is the only way to grow strong. State an experience when you stepped out of your comfort zone and things changed for the better…

Chapter 12 – Energy

"If you wish to understand the universe, think in terms of energy, frequency, and vibration."

-Nikola Tesla

Energy is found all around us. Every part of the world consists of energy. From the holy energy that made your soul to the negative energy made through the criticism of a broken person, the energy that revolves around you is constantly shifting, transforming, and refining you and everything around you. Energy is key. Learn how to increase your energy through meditation. Learn how to direct them through mindfulness, as well.

Positive energy generates at a higher frequency while negative energy at a much lower frequency. This kind of energy is the basis of all negative emotions, thoughts, and feelings that a person experiences throughout life, such as anger, sadness, jealousy, and disappointment. All of this is a part of God's plan for your experience called *The Polarity of Life*. You might not know but there are three parts of your soul – the mind, the body, and the spirit – the three essential ways that humans exchange energy: through thoughts (mind), physical touch (body), and divine spirit.

The Mind

Energy does not disintegrate or fade, it syndicates and reformulates itself while creating a strong impact on you as you move through life. The most common way of exchanging energy among humans is one-on-one transfer. The most basic and common way of one-on-one transfer is through thoughts (mind) and words. Your thoughts produce words, and words produce energy, so when a person is talking to you, their energy is trying to change your energy.

For someone to change your energy by simply using words, you have to be certain of what they are talking about. Otherwise, their words will have no effect on you. This mental state is known as Mental Fortitude and is the primary element in any connection, similar to Karma. It is important to your spiritual advancement and your ability to achieve your purpose in life. You may ask: what exactly is mental fortitude? It is your capacity to stay focused and follow the guidance of your mentors to reach your destination. In all truth, the poorer your mental fortitude is, the more you will struggle in all areas of life, and the possibility of trying anything will turn into a struggle. The most unfortunate part of a poor mental fortitude in a soul is that the weakness is self-inflicted since your soul allows the words and views of someone else to redefine how your soul perceived its spiritual self. A strong mental fortitude never allows anyone to alter their views of the marvelous beauty that created them which is the basis of your spiritual self.

The Body

Physical contact is a very powerful way to transfer energy. While the energy produced from thoughts and words can only be transferred if you invite it, the energy transfer that takes place through physical touch is frequent. There is no observation required.

Similar to every other aspect of the world, here are a few elements to consider for energy transfer.

- To touch a person in a way that is not helpful to their spiritual growth is incorrect. To touch a person to satisfy your desires instead of theirs is immoral.
- To use your body to help the broke, to protect the afraid, to heal the wounded, or to secure the unsafe

builds positive energy that is instantly shared between the parties and everyone else involved.

The Spirit

Another way the energy transfers is through a spiritual channel, also known as the Chakra system. Though positive energy can act to revive a chakra, negative energy can hinder, block, or clog a chakra. For example, when someone expresses love for you, the emotions you feel in your heart are created by the energy flowing into your heart through the core chakra. If someone tells you that they don't love you anymore, you strongly feel the emotion of rejection in your heart chakra the same way as that energy moves through and into the core of your heart.

What Is Mass Energy?

The larger the number of people, the stronger your energy becomes as it looks for similar energy and adheres to it, combining and redefining its vibrational aspect. This is known as Mass Energy. For example, consider a music concert. The vocalist of the rock band tells you that there is nothing more nerve-racking than singing on the stage in a space full of huge crowds. This happens because there is the same energy of thousands of admiring fans. Admiration is strong energy because you are giving away or sharing your adoration, your joy, and your love to and with someone else. So when the vocalist is singing on the stage and has thousands of people appreciating them, the energy is overpowering.

Since the universe needs polarity to maintain balance, this is how negative energy moves through a crowd of people. This is basically how riots take place. The more people who participate in negative or threatening energy, the more overpowering and stronger it becomes.

When you place your trust in your core, you are basically pushing negative energy out of your body. If you want to make the world a kinder and happier place, you need to start taking ownership of the energy that you are putting into this world. Be kind when interacting with others. If the polarity causes you to stop while you are on your spiritual journey, discharge the energy generated from your negative misunderstanding of the situation so that it brings no harm to anyone else.

The easiest way to do that is through meditation since negative energy requires to be reconditioned before you send it into the world. Recognize the energy and focus on it. There is no need to be afraid of it. You produce it and you control it. Second, hope for the world to change your negative energy into a positive one. You can use many imaginations to make this possible. For example, the white light changing your dark energy into white energy. However, do not visualize your energy being released into the world without any modification. Once you successfully visualize it, send it into the world and don't think about it. You no longer have control over it.

It is surrounding you at all times and is in constant movement, defining and restructuring itself. The energy you welcome in your life, the energy you let define you, is totally under your control. You simply have to accept ownership of it - the energy you allow into your heart as well as your life. Always remember to protect your core with the diligence it deserves. Why? Energy affects how people interact with each other through bodily cues. This is the reason why 80% of communication is non-verbal – the energy that is shared with another person you interact develops a certain tone of voice and specific gesture as well as a posture that makes the entire conversation.

Energy Is the Most Important and Valuable Resource

Energy, at its core, is considered to be the most important and valuable resource. However, it gets depleted from usage throughout the day. It also gets depleted when taking big, life-changing decisions and spending a large chunk of time thinking of and doing mundane things.

It becomes difficult to focus on important tasks when bombarded from every side with various distractions – from social media to work emails and pressing commitments. All of these and more distractions are enough to make a person lose their vision as well as willpower to do things we should be doing.

Wait … what? How does energy correlate with willpower in the first place? Willpower has gotten a lot of psychological hype these days and for very good reasons. It is considered an essential attribute for people who want to be more successful and focused. It helps to achieve your goals and dreams. So, what is it exactly?

Many consider willpower to be a muscle that you exercise and therefore get better at it the more you do it. Others consider willpower to be solely a matter of energy, which is depleted every time willpower is used. Willpower is confined. Every small decision you take gradually decreases your energy and your ability to take a good decision. This is the reason why Facebook CEO, Mark Zuckerberg, and Steve Jobs always wore the same style of shirts so that they could use their willpower and energy to make other important decisions. Opposing to a known belief, willpower is not a natural characteristic that you are born with or without.

Instead, it's a complicated mind-body reaction that is conceded by stress and sleep deprivation and can be reinforced through certain activities. You need to be cautious about using energy properly. You need to be aware of the emotions that overwhelm you the most and the contemplations of your questions because they define who you were yesterday, who you are today, and who you will be in the near future. Learning to meditate and living mindfully simply add on to the frequency of your vibration, altering the energy waves that your mind generates and so altering the life you live.

By simply being mindful, you start listening to your gut using your perception which is the ultimate superpower that allows you to be at the right place at the right time. What most people consider luck or coincidence is not different than the decision you deliberately make by following your observation. Nobody really teaches you how to use your sixth sense as a kid, and so you end up neglecting it. The same happens with creativity.

You know it's there but you don't realize it or give it the importance it deserves. Knowing how to use your perception and following your sixth sense can help you along your journey on many events. It even has the ability to save your life. Many attempts have been made to understand the correlation of our energy with our action and the decisions we make using our perception or intuition. One such attempt is an experiment, which is as follows.

Emoto's Water Experiment: Power of Your Thoughts

In the early 1990s, Dr. Masaru Emoto conducted a number of experiments observing the physical impact of words, prayers, music, and surroundings on the crystalline framework of water. The researcher hired a photographer to click pictures of water after being subjected to various factors and consequently frozen so that they would make a crystalline structure. The outcome was nothing but remarkable. The watermarked with positive affirmations was far more symmetrical and appealing than that marked with dark, negative phrases. This noticeable evidence is shocking. If the thoughts and words that come out of you have this impact on water crystals, it is astounding to think of the effect it could have on people and situations that come in our lives.

Where Do Humans Get Their Energy from and What Do They Do with It?

Regardless of whether you communicate with people or not, there's no denying that somewhere you've felt the energy of another human being. Somewhere along the line, somebody has had the capacity to change your temperament without saying a word to you. Perhaps, they lightened your mood with a gentle grin or made you feel disgusted by disobeying you. In any case, I can guarantee that you have felt the impact of another's energy at some point in life. Every living thing has a vibe, and this field of energy radiates around you.

Have you at any point advised somebody to escape your personal space? The sentiment of somebody being in your air bubble is a sign that they are lounging in your energy field. We trade energy with individuals in a huge number of ways, and more often than not, you don't even realize it.

- Handshakes, fist bumps, high-fives
- Hugs and kisses
- Talking – words hold a vibration, they also are energy-based
- Assaulting somebody with your thoughts – otherwise called a mystic assault
- Laughing with somebody
- Crying with somebody
- Text messages, telephone calls, web-based life
- Pictures
- Online journals and sites
- Sex

Is it true that you are someone who gets drained rapidly by large groups of people? Assuming this is the case, this is an indication that your energy is available to everyone around you. You may take their energy, or they might take energy from you inadvertently.

In case you are an individual who everybody calls for counseling, and you are continually worn out or feel depleted, it is more than likely an energy trade issue. The same goes for physical associations, for example, hugging, kissing, and sex. These are evident types of energy trade and can be either depleting or extraordinarily satisfying. In case you're giving your energy out to somebody who doesn't give it back to you, your energy won't be renewed.

Karmic connections are something how one's energy may be depleted by another. It most likely feels depleting in light of the fact that you are giving them the power to take your energy for nothing. This does not mean that they need to indicate love and warmth in similar ways that you do. Yet, the measure of adoration they have for you ought to be about the same.

Do you know about energy vampires? These individuals take, take, and take, and once in a while give back. They are somebody who continually grumbles and lives for the most part in a negative vibration. Fundamentally, they increase their energy by benefiting from others. Watch yourself cautiously around these individuals. More often than not, they don't understand but they are doing it.

Your intent ought to be to connect with the individuals who are living in a high vibration, individuals who lift you up and feed your spirit. Associating with individuals who adore you the same as you cherish them will make you feel charged and revived. This is not only in sentimental or sexual connections, but it also goes for friendships, associations, family, and even business. To guarantee that your energy is not being depleted, set the purpose to carry on with a healthy lifestyle. Whatever you are putting there, ensure that you are getting the equivalent or greater amount back.

- Raise your vibe.
- Guard your energy.
- Help people raise their vitality.
- It is ideal to do it in a specific order.

You May or May Not Be Mindful of People's Energy

Some people release positive energy and others negative. A person's energy is a blend of their past, their mindset, their powerful thoughts, their values, and their observation of the world. Sometimes, that energy is easily identified, while other times, it is just a like or a dislike of a person you meet.

Positive people are generous, compassionate, loving, kind, and sympathetic. You genuinely feel safe, happy, and calm in their presence. Their aura is welcoming. On the contrary, negative people are critical, judgmental, and unhappy. They like to bring others down. You automatically feel insecure, unhappy, and stressed around them. Their aura is not welcoming at all.

The important thing to consider here is that energy has polarity, and where there is one type of energy available, you can easily swing the meter to the opposite side. Remember, you have the power to shift from negative to positive. Here is how:

- Do what makes you happy, what ignites your inner spark, and what makes you feel good and motivated.
- Do more of it.
- Listen to your mind/body.

If you have an intuitive feeling about something, follow it. Sometimes, your gut feelings are dangerous signs and sometimes they lead you to better things. Either way, your body is a route for your higher self to communicate with you, so pay attention to those red or green signals and don't try to second-guess them or neglect them.

You bigger self can clearly see the bigger picture. However, what happens if you choose to ignore your gut feelings? You will be unhappy, in a state of resentment, frustrated, sad, miserable, and angry. Always go with the feelings that feel good and think about the ones that bring a bad sign. If they feel wrong now, then you can be certain that they will be even worse once you cross the line.

See the Good in People

Some people are very hard to deal with. There is no denying that. However, you do not have to let your negativity to influence you. Moreover, once your association with them is over, you do not have to carry the negative energy with you. You do not have to let them bring you down. You do not have to lower your vibe to their level either. You can choose to slide the negativity. Instead of blaming, criticizing, or judging, you can try to:

- Compliment them.
- Be sympathetic to the inner pain that is causing them to act rudely.
- Let it go.

You Have Control over Your Energy

You see, you are influenced by other people's energy, but to what extent is up to you. Eleanor Roosevelt quoted: *"No one has the power to make you feel inferior without your permission."*

The same idea applies to enticing feelings of anger, sadness, and worthlessness. It is your choice if you want to consider someone's words as the gospel or just a statement. It is similar to a temperature gauge of your water tap. Both sides have water, except for one is hot and the other is icy cold.

Let's apply the same concept to energy. One end is positive, high-pulsating energy that causes everything in your life to go smoothly. The other end is negative, low-pulsating energy that pushes everything in your life to resemble a series of problems and conflicts. If you ever find yourself in a situation you do not like, uplift your energy as high as possible toward the positive end of the spectrum. The more you get better at this, the more you will uplift your vibration, progressively altering your values and therefore changing your situation.

Your Doodle Page

Does uplifting your energy help you when you don't feel up to the task? Write your experience below:

Chapter 13 – Distractions

"One way to boost our will power and focus is to manage our distractions instead of letting them manage us."

-Daniel Goleman

You all are familiar with words *distracted driving* or distraction in general. You all are familiar with the car accidents caused by a teenager or an adult who was texting while driving. You all are familiar with the problems of many children to stay focused at school. You can point to several other problems and reach one conclusion - distraction is the root of all problems.

Your attention is divided into so many different directions that you do not get to focus on any one thing. You know that distraction can make learning difficult, but they are also a natural part of life. People have been dealing with distractions since the beginning, but these distractions and disturbances have been changing with time and exceeding in number. Thanks to evolution, the human brain has become more advanced yet complex. Also, the ways in which you record, perceive, and remove distractions have certainly evolved and progressed. Although this *Age of Information,* also known as the *Age of Distraction* may have made you more connected and learned, it has also made your life more hectic, chaotic, and, of course, distracted. Research is showing evidence that the brain is not able to handle the amount of information you receive, and your ability to disconnect from the external environment and connect with the present moment is declining. If you have ever come across the documentary *The Distracted Mind*, you would know that there are a variety of connections between the environment and the human brain.

The distraction that can negatively influence your ability to focus and be present at the moment can be divided into two classes: internal and external. The distractions such as daydreaming, procrastinating, and lazing around the house are examples of internally created distractions. On the other hand, distractions such as multitasking, buzzing phone, and loud co-workers are examples of externally created distractions. Here are short examples to illustrate the distractions. While reading newspaper, if you think a cup of tea would be a good idea or hope that it rains at the very moment, then internal factors are the reason for your lack of attention while reading.

Likewise, if your phone is buzzing or your baby is crying while you are trying to finish a presentation, then external factors are at work here, distracting your attention. Your attention explains the way you perceive things. It also allows a mental or rational control that helps you work properly. When distractions take control, you exceed the capacity of your cognitive power and your everyday chores are negatively affected. In short, distractions reduce the quality of your life.

Every day, emails, notifications, irrelevant advertisement messages, aimless browsing on the internet, early deadlines, and dozens of meetings, appointments, missed lunches, ignored dates, forgotten birthdays, and a packed schedule simply add up their compounding weight which later replicates in your feelings of remorse and regret.

Your time in this world is limited to a few years. How you use it really matters. Distractions take that precious time away from you, make you lose the sense of your purpose and direction, hinder your way toward your dreams and goals, and make you miss out on life opportunities. This *Age of Information* has trained you to believe that you need to engage in every piece of information you are introduced to and utilize that information as much as you possibly can in your daily activities to make the most of your life. However, if you ponder over it, constant running, moving from one task to another, and breaking your attention into hundreds of different things are barely equivalent to living a life full of joy and fulfillment. If you feel that your life is passing too fast, it is a clear sign that you are distracted, for too long, from the things that are important and deserve all your focus.

To live a happy life, you need to focus on the things that matter the most and cut off the aimless distractions that lead you to nowhere. Here is a quick everyday exercise you can do to prevent distractions. Think that you have only one day to live. How would you like to spend your time? Doing nothing or getting stuck in multiple things and not being able to complete even one task?

Once you identify where your real priorities lie, turn your entire attention toward them and put all your efforts and resources to achieve the things that make you feel proud and satisfied. It seems obvious that if you learn how to focus on one thing only for a longer period of time without falling in the distractions, then you will achieve more and so be more efficient. Distractions are everywhere especially nowadays when you are in an era where energy currency is less important than money currency and thus, people lose their attention more easily than they lose money. Deleting social media was definitely a big step and helped me a lot to stay in contact with nature. I then had a clear purpose in my mind. I also know that how I feel in nature is just way better than any other feeling in any close space. I really created a relationship with nature and that's funny because growing up in a big city I was always afraid of nature. Now I live in the most dangerous country for animals and I found myself climbing trees next to poisonous spiders.

Tired of Distractions Hindering Your Productivity? Here's How You Can Remove Them

Your entire life is composed of years, months, weeks, hours, minutes, and seconds. Although a minute or an hour does not seem like much, the impression that you can waste a few minutes is the basic and the biggest lie you ever tell yourself. Life is moving fast, time is flying, and nobody is going to wait for you or feel sorry for you because you could not make it to the end point, engrossed in distractions and useless mess. If you are not mindful, your distractions will ruin your life before you even know it. There are numerous distractions occupying the front seat of your life.

Eventually, they will take over the steering wheel too if you let them. They always promise outstanding results and great effects. However, what they really do is prevent you from doing your best and achieving your goals. You have no option but to remove them from your life if you truly want to achieve your dreams and ambitions. Here are 11 easy ways you can declutter your life from all the distractions and become more productive.

Remove Unhealthy Habits That Hurt Your Well-being

Take care of your hygiene, diet, and overall well-being to boost your energy. Turn off the television when you are working. It is even better to move to a room that has fewer distractions. This usually works well. Set yourself a bedtime routine that will help you rest well. Hire a trainer who will help you stay on track with your exercise.

They will not only set a workout routine for you but also plan a healthy diet. These simple actions will set you with a clear mind and energy to get into the right phase. They will push you to appreciate both physical and mental health. The negative voice from the haters and the critics will not reach you that easily anymore once you enter the state of perfect health and simplicity. Do not forget that you cannot get far with a broken mindset. You will have to nurture it and prepare it for the challenges to come. Being an achiever in the long term is what you truly want, but getting tired quickly or getting distracted is what you usually get without good health, sleep, and focus.

Declutter Your Mind

A number of voices, text messages, tweets, notifications, and bold content distract your attention all the time. You hear your favorite song on the radio and cannot stop singing to it. You cannot even hear your own voice over it continuous replaying in your head throughout the day. The first step you can take to remove this is to realize that you are running on autopilot mode. Next, turn it off.

It is not easy to restart the natural process at first. It is embedded deep inside you. It all depends on practice and hard work. Start working on your desires. Focus on the present and what is in front of you. Making that presentation of yours will be much easier if you get into the flow. Consider the impact you will make if you manage to finish the task on time. Think about the satisfaction you will get and the extra time you will have on your hand to do other important things. This is the best prize and will help you with future tasks when you are subjected to the same work pressure. Avoid distractions. Focus is your ultimate blessing. Make sure to use it well.

Plan Out Your Day before Starting It

When you wake up in the morning, right before you start your day, spend a few minutes in making a schedule for your entire day. One easier way to do this is by utilizing different time management tools. Take a moment to identify your priorities and realizing which tasks are more important and require urgent attention, and which tasks are not so urgent yet important so you can delay them for later or eliminate them altogether either.

The former may be more complicated since they are urgent, albeit unenticing, and boring like answering phone calls, responding to emails and clients' queries because you do it every day and you have become familiar with the routine. Guess what? It does not necessarily have to be this way. You can take control and make a calculated decision of how you are going to react when they come at your door with concerns. Once you have mastered it, hold on to it and religiously follow it.

Organize Your Workplace

When you are confronted with a difficult or lengthy task that involves your complete focus, organize your workplace desk so you can avoid as many distractions as possible. Breaks are not bad in all reality. They are the intentional de-concentration that may decline your productivity. Clear the wall in front of you and remove unnecessary material from your desk, except for the essentials that you will need to complete your task effectively.

Declutter your office and work area to allow the free flow of energy – brainwork and thinking like emptiness, coordination, and balance. Also, tend to your physical needs. Make sure you are well fed - have water to avoid dehydration and light snacks in case you feel hungry. It is good for your body and spares you the extra visits to the cafeteria with high-calorie food that will induce sleep and laziness.

Don't Get Too Attached to Your Computer

The biggest distraction is the unstoppable flow of emails and information in front of you. You receive a ping sound every time there is a new email. There goes your attention down the hill, requiring another 20 minutes for you to get your focus back to the original task. Curiosity wins every time, so grow a cold shoulder and turn off all devices completely. Start afresh. There are several new and unique ways to deal with distractions, such as social networking apps. A famous app called *Anti-social* blocks all sorts of social media interactions and enables you to become more productive. It automatically blocks sites that you waste time on and cannot seem to turn off. There are also other useful apps that will keep track of how much time you spend on your computer or individual sites.

Set Time for Yourself

Remember the second most important factor of the mystery here - time. Setting time periods for different tasks makes them more significant and less abstract. After you sit at your desk, make a list of tasks and allot time periods. Do not worry if you find yourself behind your schedule. It is only there to provide you with direction and assist you in future planning. This habit makes your day limited and adjusts your workload within that time frame if you can keep a check on every activity of yours and avoid procrastination.

Strengthen Your Attitude

To avoid all sort of distractions, align your strategies to your tasks. It is easy - pretend as if you are being watched by your supervisor and your task has a nearing deadline. It has been proven that your performance improves greatly if you know you are under evaluation or being watched. In fact, you are evaluated at all times, both by people or by life in particular. Irrespective of you doing well in the field of your choice, it is based on your performance over a significant period of time, usually over a year. A year is then fragmented into months, weeks, and days.

Meditate

Meditation is a famous technique for relaxation and avoiding the stress that can knowingly enhance your ability to stay focused. Focus allows you to pay attention to one task at the cost of all the others, which can be problematic in a world that primarily stresses on multitasking and success. Adding on to your ability to focus can nurture creativity, boost problem-solving skills, and reduce the stress linked with handling more than one task at the moment. Most people are restless. Sitting in the same position is a difficult task for them, but it can help them stay focused by putting them in control of their physical movements. Get familiar with your surroundings, but do not focus too much on your breathing pattern. Close your eyes and try not to move too much. You will find your focus being deterred by itches, hairs tickling, and bones aching. Unless you experience pain that is beyond your endurance level, do not give up. The focus you develop from meditating will help you implement it in all spheres of life. That is the reason why meditation benefits you in unique and numerous ways.

Meditation = Attention Regulation

I genuinely feel grateful now as I realize that joy and inspiration go well along with each other. You can substitute all the addictions you have, even the least significant one, by achieving a state of mind that elevates you to a superior level and helps you see things from different perspectives.

Close All Doors

The guru of American horror, Stephen King, and a very hardworking, creative writer, suggests in his book *On Writing*, *"If you can't do it literally, do it figuratively. Tell everyone you're busy for some time and ask them not to disturb you. If you're at work most of the time and working instead of conversing with co-workers, you'll actually have a lot of extra time on your hand, which will allow you to work faster and be more effective."*

This indicates that you turn off your phone. If you cannot turn it off, at least, mute it for a few hours so that nobody gets in the way of your productivity.

Plan Your Tasks

Managing and planning your tasks are the initial things that are taught in leadership classes. If you can implement the simple rules, your progress will become noticeable and work faster and effectively. But first, you need to deal with the bigger and the most important tasks. Initially, they may be overwhelming and challenging, but you can break them into smaller pieces.

You have probably heard the famous saying, *"You eat an elephant one bite at a time."* Surprisingly, it works. Take baby steps and do not let your fears and concerns distract you from giving your best. In all reality, they do not exist. They are simply wreckage of your imagination. You may sometimes get too overwhelmed by the small details. To get it out of your way, do the contrary. Combine and put together some small assignments and complete them all in one go. It is crucially effective if the tasks are of similar nature, like responding to emails, answering phone calls, or faxing important documents.

Go the Extra Mile

You must have heard multiple times that there are no traffic jams on that extra mile. To be honest, traffic is the number one time killer these days. But, if you arrive one hour early and leave one hour later than most people, you will not only save yourself from the traffic but also get more work done. The quiet office will not be a distraction and will allow you to be more productive. In other words, you will have more time on your hands.

Before you go about on your next task, think about why you read this book in the first place. Well, you did it because you wanted to become better than what you already were. Remember the historically true Einstein's quote: *"Insanity: doing the same task over and over again and hoping for different results."* If you simply go on with your everyday routine and forget what you read here, the distractions are bound to win and you lose.

Ask yourself what is it that I can do right now to implement at least one of these 11 pieces of advice. Is there anything more I can do to add on to my life and become the person I aspire to be? You will find the answers within you and will be surprised at how you were being let down by distractions when you could have easily developed focus by simply working on your abilities.

As said by Adam Hochschild, *"Work is hard. Distractions are plentiful. And time is short."* So, it makes sense to make the most of what you have.

Your Doodle Page

Has any of these tricks helped you avoid distractions and restore your productivity? If yes, which one was it?

Chapter 14 – Communication

"You can change your world by changing your words...
Remember, death and life are in the power of the tongue."

-Joel Osteen

Communication is the art of giving, receiving, and sharing – in short, talking or writing, and listening or reading. Good communicators listen actively, speak or write clearly, and respect the opinions of others. Strong communication allows people to interact face to face and in the virtual world effectively. The process revolves around both verbal and non-verbal means, consisting of speech or oral communication, writing including graphical symbols such as signs and charts, and behaviors.

In other words, communication is the science of creation and exchange of meaning between participants. Media critic, James Carey, stresses that you define your reality by sharing your experiences. That sharing is a major part of communication that is expressed through both verbal and non-verbal means. All living organisms on earth have built means in which they express their emotions and thoughts to others. It is the aptitude of humans to use words, signs, and languages to convey specific meanings that separate them from the animal kingdom. In a communication process, there is a sender, a receiver, and a message in every conversation. The receiver provides feedback to the sender's message, both while the message is being conveyed and after the message is conveyed. This feedback can be both verbal and nonverbal such as nodding in acceptance, looking away, sighing, or other innumerable gestures.

Then there is the framework of the message, the environment it is communicated in, and it's potential for interference during its sending or receiving. If the receiver can view the sender, they can understand not only the message's context but also nonverbal communication that the sender is giving off from nervousness to confidence, casualness, or professionalism. If the receiver is able to hear the sender, they can pick up signs from the sender's tone of voice, such as emphasis, emotions, and lack of interest.

Communication Is Vital to Human Life

"To effectively communicate, we must realize that we are all different in the way we perceive the world and use this understanding as a guide to our communication with others."

-Anthony Robbins

Communication is deeply interlinked with human existence. It is an important part of your life. You simply cannot think of human life without communication. Imagine how you would feel if you were not allowed to speak for a long time? Suffocated, right? In personal life, you need to communicate to deal with numerous concerns and problems of everyday life. In professional life too, it is communication that assists you in building healthy relationships and trust among co-workers.

Speaking and talking are not the only means of communication. It can take place in many forms. Sometimes, you communicate by *talking* about your ideas, thoughts, and emotions. At other times, you hope to communicate through verbal or nonverbal modes. Whatever form you decide on, getting the message across to the other party is what communication is all about. Communication is a dynamic and ongoing process and moves in a cycle. You can explain it as a common meaning between two or more people. The shared meaning rises out of the person's experiences, background, education, and social life. Similarly, in experiences, background, training, and social life lie successful communication among individuals.

It enables you to understand others around you. However, your inability to communicate well can cause a lot of problems both personally and professionally. Think of a day without communication. You can feel the emptiness it would create. Can you ever let go of the fact that it is your ability to communicate verbally that differentiates you from animals? Communication helps to develop a powerful bond among participants and makes them social beings.

Knowledge is not the only requirement for success. A person may have a good amount of knowledge, but their performance is assessed mainly on the foundation of their ability to communicate that knowledge. Therefore, if you are a strong communicator, you have higher chances of succeeding in both life and business.

Types of Communication

Communication can be carried out through different means and ways. Some of these are:

Verbal

Verbal communication is the most basic type of communication. It is the kind of communication where you use words to express your thoughts and ideas. Verbal communication can occur during numerous situations such as face-to-face conversation, radio, television, telephones, or any scenario where you use speech.

Written

Written communication is where you deliver and receive information in a written form. There are several written forms of communications, such as letters, newspapers, emails, messages, etc. It has become the most popular type of communication in, what is commonly known as, this age of information.

Signs and Body Language

Your body language is another important part of

communication. Your expressions and body language are a way through which you convey your thoughts and decisions to other people. This mode of communication is often utilized when you are interacting with an unknown person. For example, you can easily tell if a person is interested in the conversation through their body language and facial expression. Similarly, you can tell if your teacher is impressed by your presentation through their gestures and expressions.

You can also guess how a person is going to react or behave by simply observing their gestures and body language. This form of communication is also observed when a father puts his hand on his daughter's head or when a sister puts her hand on her brother's arm when his result is about to get announced. These are silent gestures that represent respect, support, and encouragement.

Communication Problems

Communication has its own obstacles that stop the sender from connecting to the receiver and vice versa.

Cultural Differences

This is the first and most common hurdle in communication. When individuals from different cultures, backgrounds, and countries communicate, they repeatedly find it hard to understand each other's accent and way of structuring sentences and words. They fail to express their emotions and feelings. Sometimes, even translation fails to deliver the actual meaning of the sentence or the real expression.

Emotional Disparity

Often, when people are going through certain situations, happy, sad, or worse, they fail to express their feelings through words to someone else. They lack the confidence to say the exact words that are needed to make the other person understand their pain or happiness. Likewise, a person not going through the same situation may find it hard to comfort the other person or sympathize with them through their words.

Physically Absent

In modern times, even though you have the best possible innovation for communication, being physically absent still has its disadvantages. The reader is not always able to understand the hidden meaning and emotion in messages sent to them. In the case of written messages, the reader solely has to depend on words. They barely get to understand the real purpose behind the message. So, your physical absence makes a conversation insufficient.

Technical Problems

In today's age, technology has a lot to do with communication. There are often problems occurring in your mobile, computer, or telephone networks that may cause a hurdle to the communication.

Importance of Communication in Life

To live a happy and successful life, communication skills are an integral part of life. Successful communication consists of trust, love, compassion, bonding, consideration, and friendship among different groups, religions, communities, and people. Communication skills gather all individuals in one place that inspires growth in the society, culture, and overall economy. This is why communication skills are so important in your everyday life.

Your communication skills are proof that you are human. It is all about how you act and talk to people. It is about how you influence the people around you through your conversation. For instance, a professional speaker or a good person is familiar with the ways of communicating in different situations and with different people. They know how to communicate with children, adults, students, family members, friends, and strangers. In all these cases, the first thing they consider is respect of opinions.

When you communicate modestly with all individuals, it represents how great of a person you are. You communicate modestly not only for the sake of profits, but you also do it out of your good nature and character. People communicate with each other differently. For instance, they communicate respectfully and politely with the rich but badly with the poor. It is their personality and nature that causes them to act the way they do.

Here's How You Can Have Effective Communication

Become an Involved Listener

When interacting with others, you often focus on what you should say. However, effective communication is less about talking and more about listening to what the other person is saying. Listening attentively means not only hearing the words or the information being communicated but also acknowledging the emotions the speaker is trying to express. There is a huge difference between active listening and just hearing. When you attentively listen – when you are involved with what is being said – you will hear the simple modulations in the other person's voice that indicate how they are feeling and the emotions they are trying to convey.

When you are an active listener, not only will you better understand the other person, you will also make that person feel heard and important, which can further build a stronger and deeper bond between you both. By communicating in such a way, you also experience a dynamic process that significantly lowers stress and supports your physical and mental well-being.

If the person you are communicating with is calm, for instance, listening in a relaxed manner will help you to remain calm too. Likewise, if the person is irritated, you can help them calm by listening actively and making them feel understood. If your plan is to understand and bond with the other person, listening actively will come naturally to you. In case it does not, try the following techniques. The more you practice them, the more content and rewarding your communication with others will become.

Tips for Becoming an Active Listener

Keep Your Eyes on the Speaker: You cannot listen actively if you are continuously checking your phone or your mind is wandering somewhere else. You need to focus your attention on the moment or the experience in front of you to pick up the simple modulations and nonverbal cues in an interaction. If, however, you find it hard to concentrate on the speaker, try repeating their words in your head. It will strengthen their message and help you understand the message accurately.

Offer Your Right Ear: As absurd as it may sound, the left side of your brain contains the basic processing centers for both speech understanding and emotions. Because the left side of your brain is linked to the right side of the body, offering your right ear can help you understand the emotional cues of what someone is saying.

Do Not Avoid or Redirect the Conversation in Your Direction: Listening is very different than waiting for your turn to talk. You cannot focus on what the other person is saying if you spend all your energy in thinking about what you are going to say next. Sometimes, the speaker can easily read your facial expression and decipher that your mind is lost somewhere else. Do not redirect the conversation in your direction by asserting something like, *"If you think that's bad, let me tell you what happened to me."*

Be Interested in What the Other Person Is Saying: Nod frequently, smile at the person talking, and make sure your pose is opening and welcoming. Encourage the speaker to continue talking by small verbal comments like *hmm*, *okay*, etc.

Leave Judgment Out of the Conversation: To communicate effectively and successfully, you do not need to like the other person or agree to their ideas, values, and opinions. However, you do need to set apart your judgment and critical evaluation to understand the other person's point of view. The most complicated communication when successfully performed can lead to a unique connection with someone.

Give Feedback: If there seems to be a disconnection, evaluate what has been said by paraphrasing. *What I'm hearing is* or *Sounds like you are saying* are great ways to reflect back. Do not just repeat what the speaker has said – you will sound unintelligent and uninterested. Ask questions to inquire and improve your listening ability.

Pay Focus on Nonverbal Signs

How you look, listen, move, or react to the person talking tells them a lot about your feelings than words can ever do. Nonverbal communication or body language consists of facial gestures, body movement, eye contact, voice tone, posture, even your muscle tension, and breathing. The ability to acknowledge and use nonverbal communication effectively can help you bond with others, convey what you really mean, explore challenging situations, and create better connections both at home and at work.

You can improve communication by making use of body language – arms on the side, standing with a welcome posture, sitting on the end of the seat, and maintaining eye contact with whom you are talking. You can also use body language to improve your verbal message. Patting a sibling on the back while complimenting them on their success is a great way to emphasize the message you are trying to convey.

Enhance How You Read Nonverbal Cues

Be Mindful of Others' Differences: Individuals from different countries and cultures are bound to use nonverbal communication signs, so it is crucial to consider age, culture, religion, gender, race, and emotional well-being when communicating through body language. A teenager, a grieving widow, and a businessman are expected to use nonverbal communication differently.

View Nonverbal Signs Collectively: Do not dwell too much on one single gesture or sign. Evaluate all the nonverbal signs you receive, from eye contact to the voice tone. Anyone can miss eye contact or briefly cross their arms without the intention to do. Consider all the signals collectively to read a person better.

Work on How You Deliver Nonverbal Communication

Use Signs That Match Your Words Rather than Oppose Them: If you are saying one thing, but your body language is saying something else, you will be making your listener confused or suspicious of something mysterious. For instance, sitting with your arms crossed and shaking your head do not connect with you telling someone that you agree with them.

Adjust Your Nonverbal Cues according to the Content: Your voice tone, to be specific, should be different when addressing a child than when you are talking to a group of professionals. Likewise, think of the emotional state and cultural values of the people you are communicating with, and adjust your tone accordingly.

Avoid Adverse Body Language: Use your body language to convey happy and positive feelings, even if you are not really experiencing them. Generally, when people are nervous or sad, they change their body language to appear positive and confident to give a long-lasting and positive impression. Instead of timidly entering a room with your head down and eyes lowered, walk with your back straight and shoulders broadened, keeping eye contact. It will make you feel confident and also make the other person feel comfortable.

Don't Let Stress Interfere

Ask yourself how many times did you feel stressed during an argument or a disagreement with your partner, boss, children, or friends and then said something or did something that you later regretted? If you can instantly relieve stress and calm yourself, you will not only avoid regretful moments but in most cases, you will also help calm the other person. It is only possible when you are in a relaxed and calm situation that you are able to listen and understand what the other person is trying to say. Especially in job interviews, presentations, meetings, or first impression, it is crucial to control your emotions, think above yourself, and communicate effectively under pressure.

Communicate Effectively by Staying under Pressure

Give Yourself Time to Think: If you think you are losing your calm, stall yourself to give yourself time to think. If you are not sure about something, ask a question for clarification before you reply.

Pause for a Second to Collect Your Thought: Silence is not always a bad thing. Pausing before responding can put you in control of your words and thoughts before replying.

Make Your Point by Providing an Example as a Supporting Piece of Information: If your reply is too long or you blabber for a minute or two, the listener will lose interest. Follow one point with a strong example and engage the listener for your second point.

Convey Your Words Clearly: In various cases, how you say something can be more important than what you say. Maintain an even tone and keep frequent eye contact. Keep your body, tone, and voice relaxed when delivering the message.

Finalize with a Short Note or Summary and Then Stop: Once you summarize your answer, stop talking. Even if it makes the room silent or you feel you still have something left to say, just stop. You do not have to fill the silence by unnecessary talking.

Quickly Relieve Stress for Effective Communication

When you feel that a conversation is getting heated up, you need something instant to bring down the emotional force. By reducing stress immediately, you can easily understand the emotions you are experiencing, take control of your emotions, and act in the right manner.

Know When You Are Becoming Stressed: Before you even know, your body will let you know that you are getting stressed as you continue the conversation. Do you feel your muscles tightening? Are your hands clenching? Are you breathing heavily? Pause for a moment to calm down before planning to respond to a conversation or delay it either.

Allow Your Senses to Rescue You: The best way to immediately and successfully relieve yourself of stress is by using your senses – sight, touch, smell, taste, sound or movement. For instance, you could pop a bubble gum in your mouth, break a walnut with your fist, relax your muscles, or simply soothe yourself through a calming image or memory. Every individual has a different response to their sensory input. You need to identify the coping mechanism that helps you relax and stay calm.

Find Humor in Stressful Situations: When used at the right time and in the right way, humor is a great stress-reliever when it comes to effective communication. When you think you or people around you are taking matters too seriously, simply crack a joke or share a funny story to lighten the mood.

Be Willing to Negotiate: Sometimes, if both the listener and the speaker bend a little, they can land a mutual ground that reduces their stress level. If you think the topic of the conversation is important to the other person, let your guard low and go easy on them. Sometimes a compromise can be a good investment in a long-term relationship.

Take Time: Take time away from the situation and the person to calm yourself. Go outside for a walk, drink cold water, or meditate for a few minutes. Physical exercise or a quiet place to recollect yourself can instantly reduce stress.

Be Assertive

Direct, assertive expressions boost clear and meaningful communication. They also help boost your self-esteem and confidence. Being assertive refers to expressing your ideas, thoughts, feelings, and demands openly and genuinely while taking a stand for yourself and respecting the opinions of others. Successful communication is all about understanding the other person, not about winning or asserting your opinion on others.

Easy Ways to Improve Your Assertiveness

- Add value to yourself and your options. They are as important as anyone else's.

- Be mindful about your needs and wants. Practice to express them without stepping on the rights of others.

- Convey negative thoughts in a respectful and positive manner. It is ok to be angry and upset, but you must try to be as respectful as possible in any form of communication.

- Be open to receiving feedback. Accept compliments openly and critical feedback even more graciously. Learn from your mistakes and always ask help when necessary.

- It is ok to say no. Always be aware of your limits, and do not let others take advantage of you or your goodness. When feeling stuck, look for options, so everyone feels appreciated.

So, in the gist of it all, communication helps you to live happily, successfully, and contently not only for yourself but also for others. It promotes a positive environment and makes huge things possible. People do not care about the money you earn or how rich you are.

The fact is that you will never be able to earn the respect of your colleagues, friends, family members, or children if you are not good at communicating your thoughts and words. The quality of the questions you ask others and yourself is equal to the quality of your life as well as the ability to think well. How you communicate with yourself depends on your comfort level. In my experience, different activities such as writing and meditation are excellent tools to communicate.

Remember, communication at its crux was invented to tell people a story or even sell one. This is why we should not believe everything we hear but use our reasoning instead. This chapter is designed to make people question things and not just believe anything that is said to them.

Society is Based on Storytelling

"The universe is made of stories, not atoms."

-Muriel Rukeyser

One of the oldest forms of communication consists of *storytelling* frequently used by humans. Form small get-togethers around campfires to watching the TV together with the family, humans are keen producers and listeners of stories. Some stories are not only memoirs or guides to amuse and entertain you. They convey important values that can help build a society, as told by recent research.

Stories have been a part of the history of almost every society. They are used to convey knowledge and useful information from one generation to another. Before humans, Aeons resumed writing. Stories were told to preserve and deliver knowledge.

In societies that lack the idea of writing, there are no libraries, archives, or other ways to hold memory, so the knowledge that is collected over a generation is saved in memory and delivered orally. Regardless of their importance, you cannot completely understand the significance of storytelling or how it changed over time.

The Value of a Good Story

The new research focused on the supportive behavior of the Agta, a hunter-gatherer population from the Philippines, discovered that good storytelling helps reinforce unity and fairness. Among the Agta, storytelling is the main factor in their everyday life. Their stories transmit messages about sex equality, cooperation, friendship, and social connection. Most of the stories told by the Agta, as well as other hunter-gatherers, include talking about social norms and the accurate way to behave in a society, like the importance of sharing food, collective action, or sex equality.

For instance, in one part of their stories, the plot comprises a fight between the Sun (male) and the Moon (female). The two characters are arguing over who should brighten the sky. When their fight is over, they mutually agree on sharing their job. The sun chooses to work during the day while the moon is assigned for night. These stories are communicated by men and women who are expert in storytelling and important members of the Agta community.

Finally, researchers evaluated the level of unity and harmony in each group by having their members play a game, where each person was given several tokens, each worth a rice grain. They were then asked to either keep it or share it further. They discovered that camps with a greater amount of storytellers were more supportive, meaning that their stories may have a real impact on the world.

The research also discovered that being a remarkable storyteller is related to age factor – a conclusion that makes sense. Aged people may be thought to have a large number of stories and therefore be more knowledgeable than younger people, as they had more time to work on their performance skills. Being a good storyteller is not about being good. The study revealed that those people who were considered a good storyteller benefited in more than one way. People who tell good stories are not selfless doers. In exchange for their services, they elevated social support, which seems to increase their reproductive well-being, as on average they bear more children than less-skilled storytellers.

Stories Are a Part of Nature

If you are not a natural storyteller, how can you tell a good story? Creating a story is not that hard. In fact, you do it every day without much consideration. Humans have been communicating stories for centuries, from historical cave painting to medieval stories about their expedition to the hospital. To initiate, break your story into three parts.

- **The issue**: What problems do you identify in your field? What products or services you think you are lacking?
- **The Expedition**: How did you reach a conclusion or a solution? How did you develop your product or service from a business point of view?
- **The Antidote**: How do you think your product or service will solve your problems?

Society created this mode of communication, not only to

connect with others but also to *sell* their ideas. This is how words are used to control people. Find the meaning of life in the words and sentences that you weave, for good.

Your Doodle Page

It's true what they say, the art of communication can make you achieve the toughest of your goal. What do you think? Do you believe words and communication have power?

Chapter 15 - Living with Sense

"Life has no meaning. Each of us has meaning, and we bring it to life. It is a waste to be asking the question when you are the answer."

-Joseph Campbell

It became very clear to me that when you spread a lie amongst truth, you can manipulate people's thinking and behavior. The most valuable asset to the *master manipulators* is your brain. Your brain computes non-sense information and turns it into truth. People spread as much nonsense information on earth as possible. They aim for you never to be aware that your thoughts and actions are in direct conflict with your core values and beliefs.

They ensure that you cannot make the distinction between sense and nonsense information. They want to make sure you remain confused and never figure out why these horrible symptoms and illnesses keep occurring. Surely, it cannot be that you keep contributing to upholding a society that causes harmful effects to people's physical, emotional, and mental health - a society that destroys people's spirits and causes illnesses, diseases, and slow and painful deaths. Surely, it cannot be that you keep destroying all forms of life in the name of evolution and progress. It is time for you to recognize that the nonsense information that is peddled to you day-in, day-out has corrupted your thinking and behavior to the extent that you have become puppets of the puppeteer without even realizing it. The nonsense information has infiltrated your way of life like a disease that quietly gains a tighter grip on your thinking and behavior, eroding your values and leaving you conflicted, confused, and divided.

It is now your responsibility to become accountable and start seeing that the Emperor has no clothes on. You must root out the make-believe, the storytelling, the third-party information, and the nonsense from your lives and start living with sense. When you do this, your health will return and the earth will start to serve you again as it was meant to. The bonds with nature that you broke that served you so well once upon a time will be restored. Do not let anyone or any nonsense to stand between nature and yourself. Your values and beliefs that you hold in high regard will start to match your thinking and your day-to-day actions.

You will start to care for one another again, and nature will be restored to its pristine state. When you decide to stop harming yourself and everything else that lives on this beautiful earth, health, peace, and happiness will be restored. You can start today to restore the natural order by eating Plant-Based Whole Foods (PBWF). What nature produces is there to serve you.

Develop an appetite for fresh foods that grow organically in the ground, on the ground, and above the ground. Start to realize that anything that is not a PBWF cannot be considered food and thus cannot serve you. It is a lie. It is nonsense information designed to control your physical, mental, emotional, and spiritual health. It is there to break you down, to profit from you, and to stop you from asking crucial questions.

It is very difficult to control people who are aware and healthy. Who can see the lies when these people start to portray nonsense information as truth? It is time for us to cleanse (detox) our bodies of all the impurities we have exposed ourselves to - all the impurities that people have breathed in, eaten, drunk, or touched. Remember that these impurities have only come into existence through all the lies, all the nonsense information you have heard throughout your life. Comprehend that man-made nonsense only brings about destruction, control, and power over others. The time has come for people all over the world to start to trust themselves again and restore the broken bonds with nature and their innate wisdom. I am here to help you to be independently live healthy for the rest of your life. I think we should be all living with sense and purpose. Living with sense means following your intuition and your senses.

For example, when a third party gives you information, always ask why. Living with sense is simply explained by an example; when you eat you should be able to feel what your body needs, that's why nature is significant because you can see it, feel it yourself without having someone always telling what this and that and you just follow instead follow your instinct and find yourself the answer.

We are the people who have lost our way. The majority of the population in this world is living a life that simply does not make sense. In this chapter, I will tell you how you can effectively turn things around and start living a life filled with meaning, purpose, and satisfaction – a life that actually makes sense.

What doesn't make sense in life? *Always thinking about the failures of your past and wondering about the anxieties of your future.* These thoughts make you fearful, stressed, worrisome, anxious, angry, and sad. They only cause you to hurt.

What does make sense in life? *Paying attention to the beauty of the present moment.* Instead of constantly resisting everything and finding things to complain or whine about, accept the giving nature of the universe that surrounds you and find meaning in the smallest things.

In every small moment lies a small gift for you to discover. When you are truly present, you can accept what the moment provides you with, whereas if you are not present, you miss out on the real gifts and beauty of the moment. If you are not living in the present moment, you are never fully here; you are never fully living your life because you are always trying to get *somewhere else.*

The energy that you give to the present moment regulates the quality of your life. Every moment is beautiful in its own way. It brings joys and energy for you to connect with it. The present moment gives you the opportunity to build the foundation for your future life, whereas not living in the present moment only stops you from living to the fullest.

What doesn't make sense? *Living a life dependent on society's expectations.* It is quite expected that who you think you are and what you stand for is not exactly what you believe in, but a representation of what your parents, peers, teachers, and friends think you are. Do you not think it is absurd that you disguise yourself as someone you are not and spend the rest of your life chasing the things that the society wants you to?

Every person begins life with a free spirit but gradually gets suffocated by the society *who to be* and what the society thinks is right for you. In reality, these people do not even know who they are and what is right for them. It is no surprise that so many people are living a senseless life - a life with no meaning and no purpose. These people constantly feel suffocated and pulled down by society's expectations.

See, you are born to be free, so be you and convey your unique inner talent to the world. Letting your life be led by external influences rather than what your heart desires, is the root cause of all the problems you face in your lifetime. Trust me, you can do a lot better than this.

What really makes sense? *Offering your best version to the world.* If you really want to live a unique and extraordinary life, you must take the time and effort to discover your greatest desires, passion, strengths, and values, and then utilize them to provide meaning to your life and the society. Dig deep and discover who you are at the very core. What inspires you? What motivates you and what ignites the spark inside you? What will you dream of doing if you have no restriction or expectation? What will your life look like if there is no one to dictate you or judge you?

Take your time to discover who you really are and then give your greatest version to the world to benefit from. Find out what you love and start investing in yourself as often as possible. Do not hold yourself back. Express yourself to the world, irrespective of the judgment others hold of you.

What doesn't make sense? *Always in search of acquiring more and more.* Bigger, better, and more. More wealth, more food, more money, more time, more luxury, more power, more status. Greed and selfishness triggered by insecurity and social fear gradually infiltrate your lives. You only need one look at the global economy to understand what I am talking about, and you will know how less is never enough.

What really makes sense? *Following your heart.* Question yourself: *Why do I work?* Do you think your work to fulfill your goals helps others create meaning in their lives? Or are you on a nonstop quest to get bigger and better and possess more? If you are in search of becoming big and owning more, you will end up on your deathbed and realize that you have wasted the best years of your life running after materialistic things. Do not wait until the very end to realize that the happiness you were seeking had always been beside you and waiting for you to pursue.

Making it no more depressing, I question you: if you are diagnosed with a fatal disease, will you continue to live the way you are living right now? Will making money be that crucial to you? Will you worry about not having enough? Will you care to impress the people around you? Or will you care more about expressing yourself and helping others with your talent?

Start embracing life now. With life so brief and confined by time, I urge you to stop avoiding the things that really matter to you. Live the life you want to live. Follow your deepest desires within you to express yourself in every aspect and begin a life that actually makes sense to you.

Pursuit of Happiness

The pursuit of happiness is a famous struggle as the majority of the self-help books claim. Yet the concept is flawed. Regardless of enough advice from experts, people often participate in activities that may lessen the benefits for their well-being or even counterattack. The search for health and sense – that is, a basis on which other aspects of well-being and being healthy might rely – has been the center of attention of years of research. New research finally points to an answer often overlooked: sense and meaning in life.

Meaning in Life: An Unsolved Mystery

Andrew Steptoe, a psychology professor from University College London and Daisy Fancourt, a senior research associate together studied a sample of 7,304 U.K. locals over the ages of 50 years extracted from the English Longitudinal Study of Ageing. Survey participants answered a series of questions about social, economic, health, and physical activity traits, including: *To what degree do you feel the things you do currently in life are worthwhile?* A follow-up survey, three years later, evaluated the same characteristics again. One important question asked in the research was: *What benefit does having a strong sense of life mean a few years down the road?*

The results revealed that the people reporting a higher sense of living and meaning in life had:

- Lower divorce rates
- Lower chances of dying alone
- Increased connections and bonds with friends
- More participation in social and cultural activities
- Lesser chances of chronic diseases
- Lower chances of depression
- Lower obesity level and improved physical activity
- More positive habits such as eating healthy, exercising, etc.

Overall, individuals with a higher sense of life live a happy life. But, what is the real meaning of life? The ancient arc of consideration of the meaning of life traces back to as far as Ancient Greece. Its roots connect to the popular works of people such as Austrian doctor Victor Frankl and linger on today in the field of psychology.

One explanation, proposed by a well-known researcher Laura King, tells us, *"Lives may be experienced as meaningful when they are felt to have a significance beyond the trivial or momentary, to have a purpose, or to have a coherence that transcends chaos…"*

This definition highlights three primary factors.

- **Significance**: The level to which a person believes their life has value and worth
- **Having a Purpose:** Having goals and direction in life
- **Coherence**: The idea that your life is categorized by predictability and routine

This extent captures not only the occurrence of meaning in life (whether you feel that your life has purpose, importance, and consistency) but also the drive to search for meaning in life.

Ways for Creating Meaning in Life

Given the stated advantages, you may think: *how can I go about creating a sense of meaning in my life?* You know from the above experiment that participants who reported higher meaning in life were more in contact with their friends and family, they engaged in social activities, volunteered for social causes, and maintained a set of healthy habits regarding sleep, eating, and exercise.

Finding these qualities in yourself might be a good place to start your search for meaning in life. Several studies have already linked these factors to meaning in life. For example, spending money on others, buying them gifts, volunteering, eating fruits and vegetables, going out for a walk every day, being healthy are all connected to attaining a sense of meaning in life.

A few more activities have been reported to bring meaning to life in the short term: imagining a happy future, writing a thank-you note to a person, participating in a volunteering task, and bonding with someone close.

Happiness and Meaning in Life: Are They the Same or Different?

There is a high level of overlap between encountering happiness and meaning. Most individuals who document one also document the other. Days, when people report they are feeling happy are also the days they report finding their meaning in life. Here is a complex connection between the two. Happiness and meaning are often separated. Satisfying basic needs boosts happiness but not meaning. On the contrary, linking a sense of one's self to their past, present, and future increases meaning but not happiness.

Socially connecting with others is important for both happiness and meaning in life, but doing so in a way that boosts meaning can happen only at the cost of personal happiness, at least tentatively. Considering the long-term social, mental, and physical advantages of having a sense of meaning in life, here is a clear suggestion. Instead of pursuing happiness as an end state, making sure of one's habits and activities providing a sense of meaning might be a safer, better, and easier route to living an established and happy life.

Living a happy and meaningful life with sense and a purpose means you actually know your work and contribution, and that your life is making a positive impact on the lives of others. Having a purpose means the work or the passion you are committed to serves humanity in a greater and positive way. Living with the purpose makes you happier, content, more successful, more generous, more hard-working, more excited, and more alive than all of your peers. Living with a sense puts you on a fast track to winning the race that you call life.

Here are a few benefits of living with a sense, meaning, and purpose.

An Infinite Supply of Fulfillment

If you are seeking to get happier, which I think we all are, adding meaning to your life can put you on the right track of fulfillment. Nothing will give you more happiness than knowing that your life has a meaning and a purpose, through which you can help another human being.

Guidance, Comfort, and Perseverance through Tough Times

Tough times are a reality that you all have to go through at one point in life. All of you struggle through dark times, situations, failures, hurdles, and trials in life. You all have phases in life when you try your best to succeed but fail anyway. It is important to understand that the hard times are unavoidable.

You cannot run away from all the problems. What you can do is use your sense to guide you through tough times and support you. When everything else fails, the sense and the purpose will be the support system that helps you put the pieces of the puzzle back together.

Nothing Can Motivate You More than Having a Positive Effect on Other People

Being mindful that there are people who depend on you will keep you motivated to keep moving forward, keep persisting, and keep determined. Knowing that your life is worth it will push you in the right direction of hard work, healing, and recovery from all your problems and trauma. In the end, you need to remember one important thing.

The world with all its distractions, the media with its carefully-formulated script will try to direct you toward their idea of how life should be lived. Do not cave in to the lure of materialistic pleasure and nonsense information peddled by the media and hawkers of consumerism. It will not bring you happiness or meaning in life.

In fact, you will lose your meaning in life and live each day without real, permanent, and wholesome happiness. I envision a world where you and everyone around you unlearn what is taught to them and find their meaning of life and what they want the most. It could be anything, a simple life, a sense of purpose, uncluttered faith, or happiness.

"The purpose of life is not only to be happy. It is to be useful, to be honorable, to be compassionate, and to have it make some difference that you have lived and lived well."

-Ralph Waldo Emerson

Your Doodle Page

Do you have a sense of purpose? If yes, what is it and how does it motivate you? Explain below:

Chapter 16 - Acceptance and Forgiveness

"To err is human, to forgive, divine."

-Alexander Pope, an Essay on Criticism

Sometimes in life, you hold onto sad memories and regrets of your past for the actions you might have done, for the words you might have said, and for the people you might have hurt. Time moves on but sometimes you do not. I am sure all of you can think of that one moment when you made a mistake that caused someone to lose their trust in you. Life is like broken glass.

You glue all the pieces together, despite how many cuts and bruises your fingers get in the attempt of doing so. Sometimes, you hurt yourself more by trying to mend things. Sometimes you cross boundaries, and no matter how much you try to backtrack, nothing changes. You try to hide things to protect the people you care about, not wanting to see them hurt. You do not tell them if someone speaks badly of them. You feel you would rather hold the secret in your heart than watch them go through the pain of what people are saying.

Sometimes, you even lie to yourself. You do things you know no one will approve of. You try to justify your actions as you look at yourself in the mirror. The fact about lies, however, is that they eventually come out. So, how do you deal with the things you are constantly running away from - conclusions and tragedies that never really get closure or goodbyes without explanation? You see, it all starts by forgiving yourself for the past. Sit down and take a moment to accept what has actually happened.

Accept full responsibility. Accept that you may never get apologies from a few people - the apologies you think you deserve. Accept that you may never take back the words that you used to hurt someone. You simply cannot think about a mistake you made and let it get to you. Let it tear you completely apart.

Do not forget that if you made no mistakes in life, you would not be the person you are today or would not learn the things you have learned. As humans, you strive for learning, taking baby steps, one at a time, moving forward gradually. While a few things get ruined and destroyed in the process, other things are reinforced and built stronger. You definitely cannot undo the past, no matter how hard you try. As a human, you can take a look at yourself in the mirror, own up to the mistakes you have made, forgive yourself and others who betrayed you, and seek forgiveness where you need to. There are chances that some people will not accept your apology, no matter how many times you say and how much you mean it. When people are on their deathbed, they have a lot to regret – the relationships they did not try for while they had the chance, the opportunity they did not avail, the mistakes they did not forgive themselves for – and they die with the remorse that ate away at them for so long.

It comes easy when thanks to mediation and mindfulness you see anger or negative emotions as a train, and you have the free choice to get on that train or wait for the next one. Playing professional soccer means having to deal with a lot of kick and people that are trying to hurt you. I learned how to forgive them and use my energy to make my team win. Same when I make a mistake myself I learn how to forgive myself and see in the mistake a great opportunity to learn.

You must learn to forgive yourself for the mistakes, irrespective of how small or big. They made you exactly who you are today. Believe it or not, you are stuck with yourself for the rest of eternity. It is time to make peace with your past and move forward.

Forgiving Others – a Difficult Thing to Do

"True forgiveness is when you can say, 'Thank you for that experience.'"

-Oprah Winfrey

One main thing that many people have a hard time with is forgiving others when they have them. You may be struggling with the same thing. People can be very cruel with their words or actions. You might be vulnerable to be hurt in this way. Especially when you are a child, you feel vulnerable to the adults around you. You have no power, no authority, no control, and no say in your matters. You are often at the mercy of their anger or frustration.

As an adult, you are still fragile to hurt, but you learn to hide the truth, you learn to hide the hurt and your fear. You learn to wear a mask at all times as you think you cannot walk around crying, complaining, or being upset at all times, nor are you willing to show people how vulnerable you are because you think it is a sign of weakness. As a young adult, you need to learn to forgive, as not to forgive has negative consequences for you and your health.

I learned it the hard time when I used to get extremely angry during soccer practice. Why? Every time I played, I would have the ball that someone kicked me to hurt me deliberately. This used to happen a lot. They hit me in such a way that I always fell down and hurt myself, which in turn made me angry.

However, I learned to meditate, and with time, I learned to forgive them, even when they never apologized to me. I simply forgave because not forgiving someone only creates a negative emotional and mental state that can cause disability and disharmony in your energy. It affects your well-being, your health, how you live your life, the experiences you make, and the type of people you attract toward yourself.

It is a big deal. People who do not forgive themselves or others end up being bitter, angry, or negative about life. They often have a long list of things they complain about, things that did not work out for them, or people who did them incorrectly. They end up blaming life for everything that goes wrong. They end up closing doors to all the great opportunities that life has to offer them further. However, forgiveness does not really mean acceptance.

It never means saying, *"It's okay what happened to you,"* or *"It was adequate that someone crushed you."* This is where most people often get confused. When you forgive someone, you forgive them for you, not for the other person. You forgive them because you do not want karma coming for you or resentment blocking your view. It usually ends up breaking you from the inside, and you walk around being angry or sad at the person who hurt you. The other person may even have no idea or clue about what has happened. This is why it is important to forgive for yourself, for your well-being and not for anyone else.

Accepting Becomes Easy

"We must let go of the life we have planned, so as to accept the one that is waiting for us."

-Joseph Campbell

Acceptance is about accepting that something has happened. You obviously cannot reverse time. You obviously cannot change things that happened in the past. All you can do is accept what has happened and see what you can learn from it. It can be difficult to learn from negative experiences but there is always something that comes out of the ruins, and you can be thankful for the lesson. The negative consequences that I have had throughout my life made me the person I am today. Without those experiences and challenges, I would have suffered less pain, but I would not have become the result and discovered myself on my journey. Learning about yourself while connecting to your happiness and fulfillment is the most amazing gift you can give yourself.

Without suffering and pain, you would have no reason to seek out something extraordinary, to discover about yourself, to learn about God, others, the universe, and so on. You must let go of the negativity about the situation. Understand that you do not hold any control of the situation anymore. In short, you can think about it and remember it but without getting overwhelmed by it or reacting to it in a negative manner.

You can think of it and talk about it like you are telling a story about someone else. Once you heal from it, you are completely detached from it or numb toward it. I am in no way saying that this is an easy task. It can take several years to do so, depending on the severity of the situation. However, it is doable for everyone to have acceptance, if this is what they want. Taking back the feelings of guilt is the biggest and hardest step. But once you do it, everything else becomes easier from that point onward. You start feeling better about yourself from that one step in the direction of self-growth. When you take back the feelings of guilt form people and life, you start seeing things from a different perspective and understand why people behave the way they do.

Sometimes, in your pain and sadness, you fail to see the damage of others and that they are incompetent of caring for you or treating you in the same way you would do for them because of their own problems. Most people do not hurt others deliberately, but your own pain can sometimes make it look like they did it on purpose. They are simply doing the best they can with what they have at hand.

Resolving something by yourself and deciding to forgive someone do not mean you have to tell that person that you have forgiven them. As I said, you do it for yourself, for your mental peace, and for your well-being. Forgiveness is an internal process, something you do by yourself, and inside yourself. If you want, you can always go back, forgive that person who did you wrong, and start working on the relationship again. You can also watch that person from afar and choose not to have them in your life. Our culture places great value on the concept of forgiveness. In some parts of the world, forgiveness is practiced even without much consideration. Forgiveness comes naturally to a few people. There are a few culturally explained meanings to the concept of forgiveness. Most of them are expressed in the way we usually talk about forgiveness. You might hear the phrase *"to forgive is to divine"* and *"forgive and forget."* At some point, you can be confused about what it really means to forgive.

- *What does it mean to forgive someone?*
- *Does it mean you forget everything that has happened?*
- *Does it mean you understand the other person's situation?*
- *Does it mean you are in a state to resolve their issues for them?*

Many books have been written on forgiveness, and no two books are the same about the topic. At the very best, you can say that a person's knowledge about what it means to forgive comes from within. It is very difficult to generalize about what it actually means to forgive. If you think you have a sound understanding of what forgiveness means for you, and you feel like you are ready to forgive yourself and those who did you wrong, then do so to move on. You should not be discouraged at the idea of forgiving your loved ones. It is a pure healing experience. However, the fact is that most people do not even have the idea of what it means to forgive. It is also true that you do not have to forgive the people around you to move with your life and create a loving relationship all over again. You can simply do that by acceptance. We have already talked about acceptance enough. Fundamentally, acceptance is to come to terms with something you cannot change. This differs a lot from the conventional ideas of forgiveness in various ways.

Acceptance does not mean you completely forget the matter. It also does not mean you magically overcome the pain that broke you from the inside. It does not also mean that you free the person of the guilt. Acceptance does not hold any abstract and complex factors that forgiveness holds. It is simply to move ahead in a positive direction toward a prosperous life. To ensure that there are no misconceptions about what acceptance means, let me introduce the five common myths that revolve around the concept of acceptance.

5 Myths Revolving around Acceptance

Sadly, many people these days have the wrong idea of what acceptance means. Here are five common myths that describe the concept.

Myth #1: You can accept all at once

This is the first common myth about acceptance. Similar to many other types of wishful thinking, people tend to admit that acceptance is plain black and white - a kind of a switch that you can turn on or off. Nothing can be far from the truth. Even if you wake up on the right side of the bed and say to yourself, *"I am finally ready to accept and move on,"* it is the outcome of a buildup of small changes and efforts over time. You may realize one day that the person or the matter has less to no impact on your life, and gradually you start to accept it.

Just like forgiveness, acceptance is also a process. There might be days when you feel you are moving on and are in the right direction. There might also be days where you feel you are drowning in your own resentment. This is a natural process and typically takes time. As fortunate or unfortunate it might appear, human beings are more complex than a simple switch. You are not a robot who can turn their emotions on or off like a switch. The desire to accept again and again is natural in any relationship. It is even more necessary in intimate relationships where the vulnerable and emotional side of you is more prone to hurt. Unavoidably, the other person can step on your feelings. You need to learn to accept the hurt they caused you genuinely to keep the relationship running smoothly. In short, do not worry about the small stuff.

Myth #2: When you accept the situation, positive feelings automatically replace the negative feelings you have

Most people think that if they accept the past, it would be as simple as drinking a magical potion that will replace all the negativity and replace it with clouds of positivity. This is not the case in any situation. Accepting the situation will not undo the hurt or the pain you have faced. It simply cannot.

Accepting things for what they are is a great way of saying that you maintain an open heart toward the other person, that you are ready to put the past behind, and that you genuinely want to move forward in life. Do not allow yourself to get tricked into believing accepting means the past has been erased. The notion of acceptance is dependent on the fact that the past is gone and, in fact, cannot be undone. After all, if you were able to change it, wouldn't you? You should be aware that your relationship is growing into something new or not. It should be different than what it originally was. Surprisingly, it is your past that had allowed it to happen. A hurtful situation does no good for either party, but it can be used as a stepping-stone. You can rise above the situation and make your relationship more amazing than it was in the beginning.

Negative emotions are equally important to you. They tell you that something is wrong and needs to be changed. Sometimes, the negative emotions indicate that it is time to move forward and look for something better. Accepting is also not about removing those negative feelings from your life. It is about using them to your advantage. It offers a way for you to use those negative feelings to make something positive.

Do not stress too much if you still have negative thoughts prevailing in your head. Let them work as a reminder that you are committed to accepting every day of your life. Accept the negative feelings again, when the past shows up. In this way, you can easily make use of good emotions. As hard and painful it may be in the short run, you can overcome anything if you make the best use of the hurt and the negative emotions.

Myth #3: Accepting means you were wrong about having such a negative turmoil in the first place

Sometimes, acceptance is connected with an acceptance of guilt or the idea that you were not right or justified in what you felt or did. This is completely wrong. Accepting does not mean that you go back and say your feelings were pointless. Remember, you felt what you felt for a specific reason. Do not feel like you have to justify your feelings or reactions. This is about both parties. In your heart, you know what is right for you and what will benefit you in the long run. Remember to prioritize yourself and your feelings. Always follow your heart's voice.

Myth #4: Accepting means the other person is off the hook

Neither you nor the other person should think that they are off the hook by accepting the situation. Acceptance does not mean that you release the other person from their responsibility. In fact, do so only when you are, or the other person is, ready to accept their mistake and full accountability for it. Acceptance means you are ready to accept the situation, move forward with a clean heart, and continue to do what is important to increase your well-being. Moving forward in this matter means both the parties need to accept responsibility and do what is better for both of them. Nevertheless, acceptance must come as a relief for both individuals. Understanding that you are ready to let go of the past and move forward should come with a breath of fresh air for both the individuals.

Myth #5: Acceptance does not mean forgetting

Even though it may be true that you are ready to move, accepting the situation does not mean that you need to forget everything about it. On the other hand, I urge you not to forget about it so you can keep track of how much you have progressed as well as what lies ahead of you.

This does not also mean that you have to think about it day and night if you are ready to move on. Accepting the situation without forgetting about it means that at some point, it will not play any part in your day-to-day life. In a way, you will feel getting more connected with life and yourself, and this time with more openness and honesty. You do not want to forget about the progress either. Try to find a balance between realizing how far you have come and how far you have to go.

"Forgiveness is not about forgetting. It is about letting go of another person's throat......Forgiveness does not create a relationship. Unless people speak the truth about what they have done and change their mind and behavior, a relationship of trust is not possible.

When you forgive someone, you certainly release them from judgment, but without true change, no real relationship can be established.........Forgiveness in no way requires that you trust the one you forgive.

But should they finally confess and repent, you will discover a miracle in your own heart that allows you to reach out and begin to build between you a bridge of reconciliation.........Forgiveness does not excuse anything.........You may have to declare your forgiveness a hundred times the first day and the second day, but the third day will be less, and each day after, until one day you will realize that you have forgiven completely. And then one day you will pray for his wholeness......"

-William P. Young, the Shack

Your Doodle Page

It's a great feeling when you accept the reality and forgive. How easy is it for you to accept and forgive? State below:

Chapter 17 - What You Really Need

"Sages do not accumulate anything; they give it all to others. The more they have, the more they give. The more they give, the more they have."

-Unknown

To live a simple life, you need first to find what you really love and really makes you grow. Then just simply think about watching a sunset, and you will find the pleasure in all the little simple things. Always try to learn new things and grow as a person and find balance with nature and yourself. You come into this world with nothing; you leave this world with nothing.

Meanwhile, you give and take throughout your life, and sometimes you fail to find a balance. You tend to gather all kinds of problems that do not serve you, physically and mentally. However, there seems to be a shift occurring lately. You hear people all around you talking about how they want to clear their houses, and their minds form all the clutter and useless things occupying most of the space.

They seem to make simplicity the theme of their life. It is time you should do the same. You all are a hostage in a big capitalist system. Marketing professionals dig into your brain, your vulnerable insecurities, and manipulate you. They persuade you that you need these things to survive and feel okay about yourself, and you will easily buy into it. If it continues for long, you will find yourself swamped with unnecessary stuff.

Apart from the unnecessary materialistic stuff, you also hold onto a lot of other things that you believe are worthy of being in your possession. On closer inspection, you will come to know that these things are just the wastage of your time and energy. You must possess the only things you really need to survive in your life.

- **The false assumption about other people's lives, especially when comparing with your own**

Comparing your life with others does not give you an actual understanding of how well you are doing. You do not really know what people are thinking, you do not know how easy or hard it is for someone, and chances are you never will. Your personal evaluation of other's lives is a forecast of one and only thing - yourself.

- **An attachment to your other life - the life of *what-ifs***

Your other life is the life of *what-ifs* that you think you could have lived if you had made alternatives or different choices. Some people also call this a parallel universe. Maintaining a home in it does not allow you to consider the possibilities that are waiting for you. It only keeps you stuck and prevents your growth.

The best way to look at the binding choice you make in life is to highlight all the possibilities on a paper. Make a journal of how your life would look like if you had made different choices, a different career, a different school, a different partner. Take a look at these choices. I assert that you will feel more right than the others, even if you have to silence all the loud voices in your head. It will simplify your life and your understanding. It will bring you to be at peace.

- **Clothes you don't wear, books you don't read, the food you don't eat, and clutter that serves no purpose**

Evaluate the things you use every day. Most of what you store is for *maybe someday*. You shop to look like someone else. You obtain the things that will make you feel what you want to feel or what someone else wants you to be. You buy these unimportant things and make them appear necessary.

There is no reason to have a wardrobe overfilled with clothes, pantry flooding with food, and you still head out every week to shop for more. There is no reason to keep storing the books you are never going to read. These books can better serve a purpose for someone else, who could actually put them to good use. Your house does not look good because it has stacked with furniture that no one uses. Simplicity is the key. Keep your homes as simple as you want your life to be simple. The clutter will only suffocate you in your space and attach you to the ideas of things that are more demanding and draining.

- **Planning the future**

Planning your future does not guarantee that it will

actually happen. You set a plan, a mental picture of what should be and what is going to happen in your life. You decide these things on a second-to-second basis. How often do you falter in future hopes? How often do you get anxious about it? How often do you end up saying, *"I can see myself doing that one day," "I'll end up here one day,"* or *"I know I'll do this one day."*

Make conscious decisions of how many times you plan something for yourself. Identify the things that make you unhappy in the present moment, and then decide what will be good for you in the upcoming future.

- **The desire to be happy at all times**

If you feel happy all the time, if you never stress over anything, if you never feel bad, hurt, or defeated, you will become mentally disabled. You will become mentally sick. You will be what clinical psychologist refer to as a psychopath — someone who does not feel regret.

Pain, similar to all other feelings, serves a purpose. It is there to tell you something. It is there to show you what is important to you, encourage you to make reasonable choices, and show you that something is not right and needs to be changed. Do not fight these feelings, listen to your heart closely, and adjust accordingly.

- **Assuming what everything means**

The things you value are the ones you have chosen, even if you have done so unconsciously. You get everything, move on, and become a different person than you thought you were. With that being said, not everything has meaning. Not everything will mean something to you or about you. What something means is how you interpret it. That is a prediction, a reflection of who you really are. The surroundings are not that meaningful. It is what you accept and feel from it.

- **Outrage**

If you feel something is not right, do not waste your time and energy sweating over it. Fight for the opposing side. You waste your own energy by releasing it on something unnecessary. Hence, it is better to keep that energy preserved by avoiding outrage and doing what is necessary.

- **Many friends**

Most of you have few close friends and a lot of acquaintances who do not add value to your life, yet you keep them in your life because it is much of a trouble to cut them off instantly. You feel responsible for something you are not. You end up creating problems for yourself by avoiding text messages, not answering phone calls, and having boring hangouts that you leave feeling tired.

Your many friends do not represent a status symbol. As the famous saying goes, *"It is better to have four quarters than a hundred pennies."* It is always quality over quantity. When you commit to a few close friends, you will find yourself investing in meaningful relationships, and stop feeling the need to impress everyone around you.

- **The desire to be in control because you think you know best**

The best part about life is that irrespective of how deeply you have convinced yourself, you are a part of all the decisions you make. It will continue to reveal as it is meant to, whether or not you have signed up for it. It is just like a three-year-old who cannot decide to turn three, but they simply do.

- **Entitlement**

This is not how you make your life simple and add value and love to yourself. Self-respect is admitting that you have the ability to work hard and achieve something great, not that you naturally deserve it. You do not deserve a new car, home, money, or a superficial life. You deserve respect and love. These are the things you are entitled to, not the shallow, materialistic ones. To put it in simple words, you are not entitled to help if you do not really need it, but you can somehow deserve it. You are not entitled to the last word or final authority from the world. You need to earn it.

- **Putting the idea into what you accept**

Love and appreciate people without thinking if they deserve it or not. If you want to make your life simple, do simpler things. If you want others to love and appreciate you, do what you expect them to do to you.

- **Put others first**

When you decide to live selflessly and offer your time to

make the world a better place for all to live, your life automatically gets better as an outcome. The only thing that really matters in life is your relationship with people. If you think about it, you will realize this is true. You build strong relationships by doing small things for others and not expecting anything in return. Do not take your relationships for granted. If you make other's life simpler and happier, your own life will follow suit.

- **Use time wisely**

Time is the most valuable asset you have in this world, so better treat it as such. One research recommends that balancing your time efficiently is one of the key ways of being genuinely happy. Some of the most common regrets that people have in their life are:

- I wish I had the nerve to live a life that I loved and not the life others expected me to.
- I wish I had not worked so hard all my life.
- I wish I had the guts to convey my feelings.
- I wish I had stayed in touch with my family and friends.
- I wish I had taught myself to live happier.

The message here is clear: focus your time and energy on the smallest things that serve a true purpose in your life and the lives of those who love you.

- **Choose meaningful conversation over small talks**

As per research, another thing you need to stay happy is meaningful conversations rather than small talks. Researchers have discovered that the happiest people spend less time on their own and more time on having thoughtful and meaningful conversations. So, if you consider yourself an introvert and do not like to socialize, you must consider stepping out of your comfort zone to have deeper and thoughtful conversations. This helps you decipher the meaning in the things that are more valuable to you.

- **Prioritize your health**

I am sure you are aware of the fact that exercise is good for you, but it may also be the key to happiness and a simpler life. A recent study in 2012 showed that people who exercise often are happier than those who do not. Exercise not only improves your overall health but it also helps you feel better. If you want to increase your chances of living a longer, happier life, then start exercising daily and eat the right food for your body.

- **Spend time in nature**

A team of researchers from the London School of Economic surveyed around 22,000 individuals and asked them to document their daily level of happiness. The study concluded that the volunteers reported they felt a lot happier outdoors in nature than those who lived in urban areas. They reported that being outdoors, near the beach, on a sunny day, next to greenery, helps you reduce stress. All these factors are directly proportional to your happiness.

- **Do something you genuinely love**

If you are still not sure what you want to do in life, here is a good place to start. Find out the things you love doing and spend time becoming an expert at them. The more you learn about the things you are passionate about in life, the more possibilities and experiences will be revealed to you. Studies suggest that these experiences make you happier than having materialistic things. This is why more and more people are turning toward minimalism – a concept that is the opposite of consumer-led materialism.

The Science of Minimalism

An experiment conducted in the 70s explored the amount of happiness of people who had their financial dreams fulfilled. The research studied that those who won millions of dollars on the lottery were equally happier to those who only met their basic needs. Money can purchase short-term happiness but you will ultimately turn to your amount of happiness before any financial profit. This places you in a malicious materialistic cycle in which you work hard to achieve long-term success and happiness through the constant splurge on material things.

How can you break this malicious cycle? First, you need to understand the origin of materialism to understand. There is actually a strong connection between low self-esteem and materialism. Low self-esteem sets the foundation for materialistic desires. It is not only about purchasing material goods for yourself. It is more about how you spend the money that determines how happy you feel. While ample research has identified the impact of income on happiness, how people spend money may be as less important as how much money they make.

Particularly, you assume that spending money on other people may have a positive effect on your happiness than spending money on yourself. Considering results over the years, it is proven that spending more money on others makes people happier than those who spend money on themselves. But, what does it have to do with minimalism? Let's explain in a quote by Colin Wright, *"What Minimalism is really all about is a reassessment of your priorities so that you can strip away the excess stuff—the possessions and ideas and relationships and activities—that don't bring value to your life."*

With this revealing itself, you find yourself doing more with less. No longer will you find materialistic things satisfying or no longer will you splurge on clothes and food. Boredom and comfort are your worst enemies. These are the two factors that push you to spend more than you should.

There is also a strong connection between happiness and social relationships. This does not come off as a surprise considering the rapid evolution. During our evolution period, we lived in small social groups, which could have been a primary cause of the evolution of language, something that made us progress as a species. This is what our experiences teach us. The ability to share experiences with other people while splurging on material things can distance you from others. When you opt minimalism, you not only make your life simpler, but you also add more to your happiness by releasing endorphins in your brain. One wonders, does minimalism create happiness? Does it make your life better? This is not entirely true. Minimalism is a topic for many people. It would be absurd to try and distinguish something as extensive and huge as happiness under one roof. Instead, minimalism is an instrument. It strips away the fat and leaves you with a new-found financial and spiritual freedom that you can utilize for new experiences that you can enjoy and share with others.

Take Action

This is not something you just think of, write in a journal, and continue with your life. At the back of your head, you should always ask yourself:

- *What kind of life do you want?*
- *What do you want from life?* And
- *What are you doing today that will set you for a better future tomorrow?*

The kind of work you do has to fit that image of your perfect life. The next step that you take has to be aligned with your future goals. The next decision you make has to act as a building block for your future. It should serve your purpose. It should make your life simple. It should help you not to become successful but happy and prosperous.

Untangle yourself from the complexities of the world. Let go of all the materialistic things and find solace in the simplistic things that the universe has to offer you. The other way around, the way most people do it is a key to unhappiness.

Your Doodle Page

Let go of all the materialistic things in your life and embrace simplicity. You feel incomparable solace. If you've tried doing so... state your experience below:

Chapter 18 - Grow Your Garden

"Life is occupied in both perpetuating itself and in surpassing itself; if all it does is maintain itself, then living is only not dying."

-Simone de Beauvoir

Guess what? We have survived the three warmest years ever recorded. It is not a coincidence. Seventeen out of eighteen hottest years have reportedly occurred since 2000, and there are no signs of reversing itself. It is ironic to consider climate change as the environmental calamity of our era, yet talking about it as an environmental problem misses the real point.

After all, the environment is not creating a problem, we are. The origin of most environmental crises, including climate change itself, is human behavior. Most humans in the modern world are disconnected from the natural world. Climate change occurs on a global scale and over a longer period of time, making it challenging for people to connect their present behavior to the ecological results of tomorrow.

The systems are connected so perfectly that you do not know where anything really comes from or where it all goes. The reaction loop is so aloof that it is almost impossible to make good decisions. This is what makes climate change so obstinate. While personal choices matter, most professionals understand that confronting a problem as big as global climate change requires thinking on a larger scale. Psychologists are among the first who changed the behaviors of people working in organizations, schools, governments, and companies to control heat consumption.

Is there hope for the world? Absolutely yes. The global environmental crisis is not a problem with science. These problems are solvable from a practical point of view. It is basically a political problem in two different ways. Firstly, the political way needs to be cultivated to make difficult choices and sacrifices.

Secondly, the national and global political structure of the universe must be evolved to create monopolization of power to deal with the crisis together. Maybe, never before in history has there been such a breach between science and politics. One issue after another, from climate change to deforestation to the annihilation of the world's sea creatures, all the scientific proof is here.

Yet, you have a political system that is almost completely failing to deal with extending problems. What is forgivable is that the scientists of the world have been warning us about the problems we have been facing for the last 40 years from air pollution to the increased use of plastic to the destruction of forests and sea animals. Sadly, powerful economic benefits like the tobacco industry in its movement to justify smoking were indeed *safe* campaigns that significantly crippled the reforms. Part of this campaign has become an effort to represent real scientists as panic-stricken agents of the dark work while industry-paid professional are realists.

The food problem is another case in many crises. Opponents of reforms have repeated over and over again the forecasts of many ecologists that there would be an intensified food shortage in the 1980s as evidence of the irrationality of the ecological movement. In all honesty, the findings of the Green Revolution are anything but transparent. By thrusting underground purifiers, dumping huge amounts of pesticides and fertilizers into the sea and crops, and replacing biodiverse seed banks with similarly designed gene seeds, there is proof that we have a new and bigger debt against the future and not a permanent solution.

The crisis of climate change today has become a part of a bigger problem. It had, in fact, gained national attention in the United States of America in the 1960s and 70s which was later neglected on the national plan since 1981 until lately. Unfortunately, these problems did not go away with time. They have been growing since then and are now more harmful than ever. We do not have enough resources to go and live in a dream world. Reality is inevitable, and the speed of change is accumulating a very harmful potential.

Plastic is Damaging Mother Earth

With the potential of being molded into any imaginable shape, strong and durable, plastic is a wonder of the world. Since the 1950s, all of us have produced an approximate of 8.3 billion metric tons of plastic. The victims of plastic usage seem to be humans on this earth. An estimate of 79 percent of the plastic made over the last 70 years has been thrown away, either into the sea, landfill locations, or into the atmosphere. Only nine percent of plastic is recycled while the rest is burned.

How Much Plastic Can You Find in the Sea?

With an average of nine million tons of plastic being dumped into the ocean every year, it is suggested there will be more plastic in the sea by 2050. 99 percent of all sea creatures on the earth will have consumed some of it. It is believed that the sea now contains more than 51 trillion micro-plastic molecules – 500 times more than stars in the galaxy. Plastic is found all over the planet, with 300 billion pieces in the once pure Arctic and a remote island in the Pacific. The abandoned Henderson Island is believed to have the maximum amount of plastic pollution in the world.

Is It Harmful?

To be honest, some kind of plastic is toxic and can interrupt the hormones that are important for healthy living. Even if it is not harmful, or not known to be, plastic behaves like a magnet for a variety of toxins and pollutants we have poured into the natural world. Plastic in the ocean looks like jellyfish to sea turtles. When it floats freely on the surface of the sea, it can disguise as a delicious snack for seagulls. Consuming this complex poison instead of real healthy food is dangerous for health. So far, it is recognized that marine pollution harms more than 600 species during what most consider as the beginning of the sixth biggest extinction of life on planet earth.

Should You Be Concerned about Pollution in the Sea?

Did you realize how humans are killing inhabitants of the sea with excessive usage and dependence of plastic? Around 92.6 million tons of plastic were caught in the sea globally in 2015, as per the United Nations' Food and Agriculture Organization. Many people do not realize how bad the situation has become. The following are some truth bombs that will force you to think more seriously about where we are headed.

- If you join all the plastic in the world end-on-end, it will circumnavigate the globe 4,200 times.
- Nearly 100,000 marine creatures die from plastic entanglement in a year. These poor creatures are the ones found, so imagine how many die in total.
- Approximately, one million sea birds die from plastic.
- The #1 human-made thing that is found by sailors in our oceans is plastic bags.

- Nearly 46,000 pieces of plastic are found in every square mile of ocean.
- It takes anything between 20-1000 years for a plastic bag to break into smaller pieces. Plastic is a material that does not break down completely. Those bags that do breakdown, turn into polymers and toxic chemicals.
- Every year, 6.4 million tons of plastic are dumped into the ocean. As a result, at least two-thirds of the world's fish stock suffer from plastic ingestion.
- Ocean acidification is a growing problem.
- Sufficient area in the ocean has been declared as *dead zones* where no life organisms can grow.

Similar to the sea creatures, plastic is penetrating into our tissues with expected harmful outcomes.

What Are We Doing about It?

The world is starting to comprehend the problem for what it is. Last year in February, the United Nations declared war on ocean plastic. Successfully, thirty (30) countries have joined hands with the UN's CleanSeas movement, including the U.K., Canada, France, Sierra Leone, Brazil, Norway,

Italy, Indonesia, Costa Rica, Kenya, and Peru. The United Kingdom while taking a bigger step in the prevention of plastic pollution has banned micro-plastic from wash-off cosmetics and skin care, such as facial scrubs, face-wash, body lotion, but not *leave-on* products like makeup and sunscreens. While an ideal solution to the problem is possibly years away, minor changes can make a huge difference.

Choosing to discard plastic straws, as most restaurants have started to do, reduces plastic waste and safeguards wildlife. Moving to reusable paper bags when shopping can also make a huge difference, as once used plastic bags are a bigger part of the problem. Being aware of the correct way to recycle common plastic is important if humans want to keep plastic away from the ocean.

Why Do We Need to Plant More Trees?

"A nation that destroys its soils destroys itself. Forests are the lungs of our land, purifying the air and giving fresh strength to our people,"

-Franklin D. Roosevelt

We, humans, are showered with innumerable blessings. God's art and work can be seen in every single creation. He has blessed us with visible and hidden blessings such as the bright stars, shining moon, songs of the birds, the winds blowing off trees, and budding of flowers that remind us there is a God who makes all things perfect and beautiful. He has made everything in the universe for our service. It depends on how we use our knowledge, expertise, and skills to obtain benefits from them.

Trees are among those most valuable and useful gifts of nature that God has bestowed on us. Not only for human beings but also for all species in the world. Trees help enhance wildlife, expand the economy, reinforce the communities, and create a sustainable future. Planting a tree has become very important in today's world, yet many people do not realize it.

Forests still occupy about 30 percent of the world's land area, yet they are disappearing at an exceptionally increasing rate. According to the World Bank, between the time of 1990 and 2016, the world lost some 502,000 square miles of forest – an area bigger than South Africa. As humans began cutting forests, 46 percent of trees have been destroyed, as per a study in 2015. Around 18 percent of the Amazonian rainforest has been wrecked over the past 50 years. Losses have been on the surge. Trees are important for numerous reasons, not only for what most think that they absorb carbon dioxide that we exhale, but also for the heat-consuming greenhouse gases that human activities emanate. Since those gases penetrate the atmosphere, global warming increases a trend that scientists refer to as climate change. Tropical trees alone can provide 23 percent of the climate control needed over the next era to meet objectives discussed in the Paris Agreement in 2015.

What Causes Deforestation?

Excessive farming, grazing of livestock, mining, and drilling report for more than half of all deforestation. Dendrology practices, wildfires, and in some portions urbanization report for the remaining. People in Malaysia and Indonesia cut down forests to make room for producing palm oil, which is available in everything from shampoos to saltines. In the Amazon, cattle farming and farms in general, especially soy plantation, are the main culprits.

Woodcutting operations that provide the world with wood and paper-related products wreck thousands of trees every year. Workers, some of them working illegally, construct roads to reach more and more deserted forests that lead to more deforestation. Forests are frequently cut down as a consequence of growing urban mass as land is built for homes.

Why It Matters?

Deforestation affects both animals and humans wherever trees are cut. Around 250 million people living in the forest and the Amazon are reliant on trees for food and income. Many of them are among the world's rural poor. In case you do not know, eighty percent of the world's plants and animals occupy the forests. Hence, deforestation intimidates species including the monkeys, Sumatran, and tigers.

Destroying trees withdraws the forests of parts of its shade, which prevents the sun rays during the day and preserves heat at night. This disruption is followed by more severe temperature fluctuations that can be dangerous to plants, animals, and us. The impact of deforestation extends much farther. The South American rainforest, for instance, has an impact on regional and maybe even global water cycles. It is primary to the water supply in Brazilian cities and bordering countries.

The Amazon, in fact, helps distribute water to soy farmers and beef breeders who empty the forest. The deficiency of clean water and biodiversity from all forests could have numerous other effects that you and I cannot even envision while enjoying a warm cup of coffee. In regard to climate warming, cutting trees emits carbon dioxide into the atmosphere and removes the potential to absorb already present carbon dioxide.

Social activists and non-profit organizations are working to combat banned mining and logging. In the forests of Tanzania, the locals of Kokota have planted more than two million trees on their small land over many years, trying to repair the earlier damage. On the other hand, in Brazil ecologists are protesting in the face of threatening signs that the government may take back forest protection measures.

It is logical for consumers to inspect the products and meat they purchase, searching for sustainably produced sources when they can. Here are a few easy ways you can be a part of the cause of saving mother Earth and creating a sustainable future for the coming generations.

Whole plant based food

Environmental Working Group discovered that red meat causes 10 to 50 times as many greenhouse emanations as regular vegetables and grains. If the grain consumed by livestock is consumed by people, they can feed 800 million more people. Apart from environmental benefits, reduced meat consumption has positive effects on your overall health and lifestyle.

In contrast to the above point, this has slightly weak statistics. It requires a lot of feed to maintain a dairy cow. Sixty-six percent of all grain calories are fed to the cows. Cow farts are responsible for all methane emanations related to human activities.

Alter Your Driving Patterns

Not everyone is blessed with the gift of being able to walk anywhere and everywhere, yet vehicles are the biggest threat to the environment. The tailpipes of your car are at street level, where you can easily inhale polluted and toxic air directly. Think of a world where you can carpool, use Uber, walk, or take a cycle.

Keep a Check on the Amount of Water You Use

Water is one of the biggest blessings of all. We use it frequently, all the time, and sixty-five percent of what you use is in the bathroom. Take quicker and shorter showers. Do not leave the tap running while brushing your teeth. Purchase an energy showerhead. Better, shower together and save water. It all helps.

Plastic-free lifestyle

Did you know that forty percent of the world's economically cut timber is used for paper? This jeopardizes the natural environment and also utilizes a ton of water. It has become cheap to print. You do it without thinking. In case you cannot even realize all of a sudden if you are paperless, think about your bank documents, the paper towels you use, the spam mail you print, and the paper you use for wrapping Christmas gifts. There are too many ways.

Shift to Refillable Water Bottles and Reusable Lunchboxes

Using bottled water and then throwing away the bottle is adding more to the pollution. Landfills are overflowing with water bottles. It is reported that three liters of water are used to pack one bottle of water. It is time you spend on steel water bottles and BPA lunch containers that last longer. If not that, a mason jar is pretty and can be used several times.

Know What You Throw in the Trash

From leftovers to kitchen scraps that can be used to make recycled items, your trash can be less full, the more mindful you are of what you put in it. Connect with your old inner soul and see how many times you can reuse or repurpose rather than simply throwing it away.

Use Your Own Bags

Before heading out on your next shopping trip, make sure you take your own reusable shopping bag with you. I am sure by now, you know that plastic bags are a massive threat to oceanic life and cause a problem to the environment. Reusable paper bags are the future.

Fix or Borrow Instead of Buying

Purchasing second-hand material is useful for the environment. One kilo of fabric produces 23 kilos of greenhouse gases. It not only helps the environment but also helps you save more. Start pondering over the things you own and become sharp about what you spend on and why. Stitch your own socks and sew your own buttons. Borrow clothes if you see yourself in two different sizes.

Grow Your Own Vegetables

Grow your own fruits and nutritious vegetables. Start by planting in your own kitchen garden. The fruits and vegetables you grow in your garden are more nutritious than the ones that travel thousands of miles and processes to reach to your nearest grocery store. By growing your own garden, you can benefit from free shade. You can use less and good quality pesticides that will have fewer chances of contaminating the environment.

Fruit peels and waste can accumulate to a lot of green waste and occupy a lot of space in your trash can. Recycle them to make your own manure. It is way better than buying fertilizer. Become creative while growing your garden. There is a potential to grow a unique garden similar to futuristic sustainable gardens that are less expensive and need less space. It does not matter if you do not have a big portion of land. In fact, you do not need any land. You can simply grow your garden in pots.

Not a fan of dirt on your hands? It is actually beneficial for your health, but if that is preventing you from growing your own garden, wear gloves. How will you ever know if you have a knack for gardening if you do not even try it?

There are numerous benefits of growing your own garden. Growing my own garden helped me find a connection with nature even deeply. I think it is amazing to see how from a little seed comes a beautiful and flavorful food that feeds not only your body but your soul. Don't eat because it is time to eat. Eat to feed your mind and soul. That seed will have all your energies and so when you eat the vegetable, then you feel more connected.

For starters, you will benefit from fresh air and sun – the natural source of vitamin D, utilizing your hands, mind, and body. Who would have thought that playing in dirt could be this fun and beneficial? Once you get on with the planting, weeding, and picking, you will get so involved in the task that you will absolutely enjoy the fruits of your labor. You can be surprised at how rewarding gardening your vegetables can be.

Here are a few reasons that you should start your garden.

It Reduces Stress

Gardening not only lessens stress, but it also helps lower blood pressure and fight symptoms of depression. A research conducted in the Netherlands discovered that gardening puts patients in a positive mood and sustains that mood. Also, it concluded that the micro-organisms found in the dirt could help boost spirits.

Improves Your Health

Cultivating fruits and vegetables is a great and simple way to eat healthier. Vegetables when grown at home taste much better than those you purchase from your local grocery store. They are not chemically mutated. They are not frozen. They are free from any pesticides. When gardening, remain in touch with nature - fresh air and sunshine. Having your garden is not only healthy for your body, but it also helps you mentally.

Connects with Nature

When you grow your garden, you increase your knowledge about what plants to grow. This means you will be in sync with different seasons. What vegetables grow the best at what temperature? Are they receiving enough sunshine? Are they getting enough water? These are actual questions you need answers to before becoming effective at planting. The best part about gardening your own vegetables is watching the seeds you sow into full-sized plants. Nature works at its best when you keep in contact with what is going on around you.

You Save Money

With the prices of fruits and vegetables hitting sky high, growing your own vegetables is a smart way to save money. You not only get a wide variety of products but they are also fresh and straight from your own garden. Gardening has always been at the core of all philosophical discussion. Adding value to the environment gives rise to all kinds of questions from the major ones to the smallest yet the most useful ones.

Take time as you build your relationship with your garden and nature. You will be surprised at how fast you reap the benefits. Your efforts of today can help to build a sustainable and prosperous future for tomorrow. Similarly, the decision you make today will help to set a path for your future generation.

Your Doodle Page

What have you done to save the environment? Every small idea counts...

Chapter 19 - Love Out Loud

"If you love someone, you say it, right then, out loud. Otherwise, the moment just passes you by."

-Julia Roberts

You cannot explain a mother's love in words. Every day, her heart is filled with a new-found love for her child. She cradles a small baby in her arms and does so without asking anything but love in return. She nurtures you, protects you, feeds you, bathes you, and sacrifices for you without a whim of cry. Her love is pure. It is purest then the whitest snow. She stays up late so you can sleep in peace.

The love of a mother goes beyond the boundaries of language, tribe, and socio-economic status. She represents sacrifice, love, encouragement, and a ray of sunshine. Of all the different types of love, a mother's love is the strongest and most powerful. The bond between a mother and her child rises as a connection bringing two bodies and soul together. Her love is eternal and unconditional. When you say that nature is intelligent, one of the things that you refer to is the bond between a mother and her child. A mother's ability to protect her children starts from the moment she realizes she is pregnant. Over the next nine months, while she is yet to see her child, he or she becomes the most precious thing in the world for her.

Babies have a survival instinct. They are naturally born with a set of techniques or tricks that urge the adults around them to look out for them and tend to them. This is called the smile reflex. However, the bond between a mother and child is quite different. It goes far from the baby's survival instinct. Similarly, any other healthy relationship in the world is based on unconditional love, affection, trust, and respect; even the relationship you have with yourself.

"So now faith, hope, and love abide, these three; but the greatest of these is love."

-1 Corinthians 13:13

The Philosophy of Unconditional Love

"Love is patient, love is kind and envies no one."

-Corinthians 13

Is love unconditional? If unconditional means you love regardless of boundaries, the other person's traits, or actions, does that not mean you should love everyone the same way? If not, how do you selectively love someone unconditionally? Maybe, the feelings you save for those you adore the most in the world are best explained as selfless love instead of unconditional love, in which you are faced with another obstacle. What happens when your loved one changes instantly and loses the features and the personality that caused you to love them in the first place?

Unconditional love is rare to find and difficult to sustain. You may ask what the difference between potential love and romantic love is. When unconditional love ensues, it is a wonderful feeling. Of course, you want someone to always love you. However, is eternal love different than unconditional love?

Unconditional love is the highest and most pure form of love. Most religions comprehend this too. This is why they ascribe unconditional love from man to God. If God were in all reality, then unconditional love would be a lot easier for Him, considering the conforming unbounded patience and act of forgiveness. However, humans are not like this. You get hurt and disappointed. These two truths can destroy even the apparently most lasting love. Maintaining unconditional love is, of course, a difficult thing. Being on the receiving end is no doubt the best thing. People want to be loved and appreciated for who they really are and what they do. However, just because you love someone unconditionally does not mean you do not bother about these factors. When you truly love someone, you want them to be the best version of themselves.

What about the bad behavior that goes undiscussed, with domestic violence and the frequently occurring inability to let go of an abusive spouse? That refers to self-destructive love. So, does that mean unconditional love is similar to self-love? If yes, the self gets in the middle for most people. In a study conducted on newlyweds to forecast the long life of the marriage, people were mindful of the failings of their partner in the early stages of the study.

The long life of the marriage was predicted by mixing this mindfulness of failings with the unconditional love they had for each other. Parental love is also one of the strongest forms of selfless love, but there, we see the child is bonded with the parent, i.e., an image, to some extent of the self. In the study of the newlyweds, the interchange is the main factor able to hold the marriage together. So are either of these types of love selfless? Think of adoption: why do people adopt? Because they care for children. They did not give birth, which is quite a big act of love in itself. But the question of how unconditionally one's love should persist? Where does love for your own self lie along the meter of unconditional love? How can you balance it with love for others? The idea of unconditional love arises from within one's own self and ability to love. The love grows inside you when you embark on adventures your heart yearns for.

The love inside you grows when you follow your heart's passion and live your best life without any regret. The love within you grows and outgrows you when you accept your flaws and embrace them when you decide to share it with people around you, with the rest of the world, when you decide to let the world in your heart and share all your love with all of humanity. You love unconditionally when you love out loud. Love out loud was an inspiration from my friend Nicole Gibson who wrote a book about that and really inspired me to love without a condition just for being able to love no matter the circumstances. Let the ego aside and be who you really are with heart and mind open; loving and being grateful for the simpler things.

You see, you do not become the best version of yourself overnight. It takes hard work, persistence, passion, strong will, compassion, and a lot of determination. You first have to be vulnerable yourself to be able to tend to the vulnerable, when you become the melody of the music everyone dances to, when you become the colors of your painting, and when you finally decide to let go of the person you are, the person the world awaits you.

That is what has been the theme of my book, to motivate you to become the best version of yourself, to go out into the world and take risks, to face challenges because you only become a diamond when you are put through extreme pressure. The purpose of my book is to enlighten you with all the wonders of life awaiting you. To encourage you to pursue your interests and see how beautifully and magically they transform you. To let you know how beautiful life is and how you should walk this race of life and open all doors with open arms.

This journey has been a wonderful experience on my own. While invigorating on my own life when I came to Australia at the age of 18 has been a life-changing experience. Writing this book has only added more to it. This book is not an ordinary book. It may lay out there on your desk collecting dust for some time, but you will find yourself reaching out for it from time to time because it is a song for your rough times and an antidote for all your problems. This book emphasizes some of the most important things required to spend a meaningful and purposeful life. From education to meditation to forgiving each other and living a stress-free life, this book has answers to all of your life queries. You see, education brings along curiosity with itself.

It questions you and makes you question the things around you. It challenges you and pushes you to look for answers within you and outside you. Some of the famous people of all times are Leonardo Da Vinci, Albert Einstein, and Nikola Tesla. What do you think all of these have in common? Their thirst for knowledge, their hunger for curiosity, and their drive for making the most of every moment.

They observed the simplicity in things and created marvelous creations out of them. Through education and mindfulness, you bring back your wandering attention which is the origin of every will, judgment, and decision you make hereafter. You simply seize the day, 'Carpe Diem' and let life take you by the course of it. A simple and easy way of letting mindfulness enter your soul is by maintaining a mental discipline with the purpose of training your focus to the things that are necessary and worthy. Mindfulness and meditation are often the words associated with each other when you talk about focus and maintaining your attention. Meditation has played a great role in my life. From helping me see perspective to becoming calmer, poised, and relaxed, the benefits of mediation have proved valuable at every step of my life. I feel like there has not been enough emphasis on how meditation affects your life.

It completely transforms the way you look at life. It prevents negative energy from reaching you. It helps you maintain a healthy lifestyle. You need to realize that negativity, anxiety, anger, and fear are simply trying to distract you from your purpose in life. Any thought that you would rather not have if you try to stop them will involuntarily trigger them and increase its negative impact on you.

Whereas, if you simply observe them as imaginary thoughts trying to waiver your attention from meaningful things, you may have chances of bringing back your attention to what really matters, and thus you will be free of their knots. You can overcome these negative thoughts and emotions by simply breathing in and out, meditating, or gaining control of yourself, and they will vanish, fade away, and blur out from your life like they never existed. Once you start noticing when your mind wanders into the default mode, you will have a chance to embrace the present moment, be mindful, and come back to the moment and live it – in fact, enjoy it. Do not let ego come between you and your goals. Do not feed your mind on negativity either. You simply identify your ego and set yourself free from its ties.

The exercise of identifying your mind and being a witness of your thoughts allows you to understand that you can separate yourself from it. What is the ego? The ego is the little voice at the back of your head that is always trying to analyze or judge what is going on around you. Every time you start thinking about the past and regret about it or even start imagining the future and desiring something, that is the ego taking control of your brain.

In this situation, all you can do is take a deep breath, straighten your back, and inhale the moment while trying to focus on the present moment. Your ego will try to escape the moment, making the future look better or reliving the memories but your ability to live in the present will help you fight it. It will bring you back to reality. The past and future are mere imaginations of your mind. The only reality is the one you are living right now in this very moment. When you are actually focused on the present, you are more responsive; you are brave yet calm. You become more conscious of your thoughts and your actions. You open your mind to all the amazing possibilities in front of you. You become aware of the details in the most unwanted things. You become fascinated by nature and the beauty you are surrounded by. You break free from all the barriers holding you back.

You offer the world your best personality, your mind, your kind words, and your caring heart. You do not let society or the world dictate your actions. You move and learn constantly. You do not let others design your commute. You thank God for the blessings He has provided you with and go about in the world living every day, every hour like it is your last.

Your experiences with nature and the outside world improve your health, your thoughts, and your memory. Your body responds positively to every action of yours. Your skin glows and feels at your very best. This process, scientific yet beautiful, marked with small details inspires you to move around and do something big with your gifts. Living through that life and moving through the tide of waves, you learn to give without expectations of receiving.

Just like the trees give you oxygen, the sun gives you warmth, you too give to the world without asking for anything in return. The science behind expectation rewards your body by the release of healthy hormones. The hormones that you need to function, love, bond, and connect with others around you. Every single part of your body, brain, and spiritual self is deeply connected with each other, making sense of you and the life you are living.

Before words were even created, you communicated your thoughts and ideas to the world. You created meaning out of the most random thing. You created intimacy and understanding of the world. All this by simply stepping out of your comfort zone, overcoming all the obstacles that life threw at you, and realizing that you were so much more than what you thought you were.

You create positive energy around you and emit that same energy to the world that attracts people toward you. The energy you create paves for your interactions, your non-verbal communication, and how you perceive the world. Every single decision you make is based on the energy you emit. You attract people who think like you, who share the same interests as you, and who are willing to share your passion with you.

This is why I always say to let go of all the worldly distractions and live a life as simple as the veins of leaves. Remove all those things from your life that complicate the process and stop you from being you and those that hinder your productivity and growth. A life dependent on materialistic belongings is a life not lived. To live a prosperous and meaningful life, you surround yourself with meaning, you give into it and what it has to teach you. You take inspiration from the greatest teachers of all times - Jesus, Buddha, and the great philosophers. You walk in their footsteps and let them guide your way to ultimate happiness and serenity.

You eventually learn to communicate your positivity to others. You understand the modes of communication between people and use them efficiently to improve your relationships and bonds with others. You are not a creature of habit. You learn to step out, challenge yourself, and do what requires more effort, risk, and hard work to prove yourself. When you are on the right path, you begin to live a life with sense, a sense of how and why, a sense of who you are and why people are the way they are. You no longer hold people responsible for their actions, you no longer regret the mistakes of the past, and you no longer blame life for being hard on you. Why? Because you understand that everyone is in the same race as you. Everyone else is trying to live life and a darn good life in fact. You not only forgive others, but you forgive yourself. You cut yourself some slack and realize that you do not have to be so hard on yourself to make peace with the present. You come out of the dark past and stop envisioning the future. You in all your senses become more mindful, more aware, and more conscious of the things and the reality in front of you.

How to Live More Mindfully

You must have noticed how quickly a destination arrives when starting on a journey, only to realize that you had not noticed anything or anyone between the start and end of the journey. Of course, you had but your mind was not present at the moment, which is a classic example of *mindlessness* or *going on automatic pilot-mode.*

We have already established how important mindfulness is, but how can you bring more mindfulness into your everyday life? The Thing is, we all fall into habits of mind and body, attention and inattention which result in our not being present for most of our lives. The consequences of this behavior are sometimes incredibly costly, causing people to miss some good things in life and foregoing important information about their life, relationships, and even health.

You can practice mindfulness to get out of automatic pilot-mode. What does it mean? Practicing mindfulness means to pay more attention in a particular way, remaining in the present moment. Remember, mindfulness knows what is going on outside and also inside your skin.

"Feelings come and go like clouds in a windy sky. Conscious breathing is my anchor."

-Thich Nhat Hanh

What happens when you start to pay attention to the world? A new beginning awaits where you acquire things and people you need the most in life. You step out of your superficial needs and rely more on the mental, physical, and spiritual needs that will assist your growth. You invest more in your growth, you water your roots, you tend to the garden of your thoughts, and you involve yourself more into the causes that will help others in their self-discovery. You become vulnerable to the needs of others, to the needs of your mother nature, and to the environment. You no longer remain quiet in the realms of your demise. You try to put meaning into things that are bigger than yourself. Most importantly, you start to love – love out loud with no barriers and no shame. This book has been my way of sharing my story of how I overcame anxiety and depression. I have shared the things that helped me get through a radical change in life. All the things that made life worth living. For example, quitting social media, start meditating every day, having a gratitude journal, stepping out of my comfort zone, reading a book a week, eating a whole plant-based food diet, and many other activities that changed my life for better.

I want to help you understand the philosophy behind every aspect of life. Let's say meditation is a way to know and communicate with yourself, like a cloud in the sky and your mind is the vast sky or thought. They can be connected but are still separate, giving you the chance to see through as trains. So you can decide if you want to get on that train or let it go. If you want to avail the opportunity of living life to the fullest, the decision is in your hands. You know that life is a race and you are not here to win it but to enjoy it.

"Life is a game, play it; Life is a challenge, Meet it; Life is an opportunity, Capture it."

-Unknown

Your Doodle Page

Don't shy away from hiding your love… say it out loud. Or else, the moment might pass and you would end up regretting. State an experience when you confessed your love and how it made you feel.

Bibliography

Bass, Randall V.; Good, J. W. (2014) *Educare and Educere: Is a Balance Possible in the Educational System?* Retrieved from https://eric.ed.gov/?id=EJ724880

By Dr. Bruce D. Perry (2018) *Why Young Children Are Curious.* Retrieved from https://www.scholastic.com/teachers/articles/teaching-content/why-young-children-are-curious/
Thorin Klosowski (2018)

Study Explains How Walking Can Boost Your Creativity. Retrieved from https://lifehacker.com/study-explains-why-walking-can-boost-your-creativity-1569838156

Sue McGreevey. (2011). *Eight weeks to a better brain.* The Harvard Gazette. Retrieved from https://news.harvard.edu/gazette/story/2011/01/eight-weeks-to-a-better-brain/

NICOLÓ DI LEO LANZA